The Story

of

Everything

The Story
of
Everything

A Parable of Creation and Evolution

JOHN KOTRE

COWLEY PUBLICATIONS
Lanham • Chicago • New York • Toronto • Plymouth, UK

Published by Cowley Publications
An imprint of Rowman & Littlefield Publishers, Inc.
A wholly owned subsidary of The Rowman & Littlefield Publishing Group, Inc.
4501 Forbes Boulevard, Suite 200
Lanham, MD 20706

Estover Road
Plymouth PL6 7PY
United Kingdom

Distributed by National Book Network

Library of Congress Cataloging-in-Publication Data

Kotre, John N.
  The story of everything : a parable of creation and evolution / John Kotre.
    p. cm.
  ISBN-13: 978-1-56101-298-5 (pbk. : alk. paper)
  ISBN-10: 1-56101-298-X (pbk. : alk. paper)
  1. Creation—Fiction. 2. Evolution (Biology)—Fiction. I. Title.
PS3611.O7493A65 2007
813'.6—dc22   2007004836

Printed in the United States of America.

∞™ The paper used in this publication meets the minimum requirements of
American National Standard for Information Sciences—Permanence of
Paper for Printed Library Materials, ANSI/NISO Z39.48-1992.

To Michael Wilt,
who found the story
and kept it alive.

To Begin

THIS is a parable. A parable is a story you lay down next to a mystery, as a way of honoring it. When the mystery is about *everything*—about quarks and bugs and spirits and stars, not to mention science, religion, and philosophy—well, that's a lot for a parable to handle.

So this one is longer than most. But it's not that complicated. There's a Speaker. There's a Story. Each has a life. Each makes a journey. The Story's journey seems almost human, which should not be surprising because stories *are* a lot like people. They are born, they grow, and they die, just like people do. They enter your life, they stay for a while, they leave. Where they go is anybody's guess, but sometimes they return, vastly changed.

"We are in trouble just now because we are in between stories," said the priest and self-described "Earth Scholar" Thomas Berry in 1978:

> The Old Story—the account of how the world came to be and how we fit into it—sustained us for a long time. It shaped our emotional attitudes, provided us with life purpose, energized action, consecrated suffering, integrated knowledge, and

guided education. We awoke in the morning and knew where we were. We could answer the questions of our children.

But no longer, said Berry, and he saw a New Story in the distance, coming our way. Nearly thirty years later, we are still in between. Maybe that's because it's hard to let the Old Story go. When you love something, when you hold it sacred, how can you show it the door and give its place to a stranger? There is guilt in the transition, and fear. You feel unclean. You feel uncertain. You betray the Old even as you greet the New.

And so, as Berry foresaw, we are still in trouble. In our schools and courts we go to war these days under the flags of "creation," "evolution," and "intelligent design." Some of us fight for the Old, others just as desperately, as "fundamentally," for the New. It looks like a war between religion and science, but it is not; it is a war between those who embrace their stories with a grip so tight they squeeze the very life from them. Look at the result of such embraces: a bloody trail throughout history of people dying—and killing—for intractable versions of a story.

What? you say. Killing for a story? Why would anyone do that? You forget: these are stories of *everything*.

Maybe if we entered the world of these stories, maybe if we went where they went and saw what they saw and listened in on their thoughts, maybe we would understand them better. Maybe we'd let them go on a long, long walk by the sea, all by themselves. I think they would like that. I think they would come back refreshed—silent and innocent, sensitive to mystery once again, absorbent, ready to find the next Speaker.

The Story
of
Everything

O N E

WHEN the great oak came down in the green storm (that was the color the sky turned just before it hit), Adam's grandfather said he would clean it up, but not right away. So don't pester him. The next day he and Adam walked out behind the barn, splashed through a creek that had turned into mud, and climbed the hill where the oak once stood, alone in its splendor. Adam walked around and under the fallen giant, pushing aside twisted branches, fingering the huge splinters and deep white fractures in its wood. Grandfather was right behind him.

"Look at the rot," Grandfather said, and Adam felt it too. It was moist and soft, and almost as dark as the earth.

For many evenings after that, Adam and his grandfather returned to the hill and inspected the tree more closely. Its green leaves started to droop, and then they turned a leathery brown, but they never fell to the ground. Adam found a squirrel's nest up in a crook and wondered what it would be like to have it for a home. He looked down the branches leading out from the nest. He calculated the leaps from one to the next. He saw himself scrambling around and around the trunk of the tree, chasing his brothers and sisters and cousins.

Then he wondered what the storm was like. Huddling in the nest with his family. Getting soaked. Shivering. Feeling the wild swaying of the tree. And then—bang! A flash, a crack, and down it would have come, slowly at first and then faster and faster, until it slammed to the ground with a thud.

It was a long time before Grandfather's cleanup started. He didn't say a word to anyone about what he was going to do or when he was going to do it. Then one morning he took an axe and a saw out to the hill and spent the day there. The next day as well. Adam could have run out to see what was happening, but Grandfather had told him not to. And while Adam wasn't known for his obedience, he knew his grandfather was up to something, and he liked to be surprised. So he stayed on his side of the barn.

On the third day Grandfather took him back across the creek, which was running clear again, and up to the hill. There Adam stood in amazement. The tree was still on its side, but all its brown and drooping leaves were gone. Smooth white circles appeared where limbs had been sawed off. The tree looked naked, but strong, like a huge octopus lying on its side, its legs frozen at angles in the air.

"Go ahead," said Grandfather.

Adam leapt onto the trunk of the tree and tiptoed, with arms extended, to the end of every branch. As that summer turned into fall, his friends came to the hill and tiptoed too. Sometimes there were a dozen of them climbing all over that great frame, calling out from the top to the bottom of it, bouncing on its buoyant limbs, hanging upside down by their knees. As evening came, they would quiet down and sit among the branches in twos or threes, legs kicking gently beneath them, awaiting the sunset. On one of those occasions Grandfather took their picture.

Then Adam's grandfather told everyone, Adam included, to stay away again. This time, however, Adam's curiosity got the better of him. He snuck out behind the barn and watched from behind a clump of brush as his grandfather leveled off the top of the stump, chiseled out the rot, and carved . . . a chair. A throne, almost.

In the days that remained that fall, Adam and his grandfather would often go out to the fallen oak tree. Grandfather would sit on the trunk and Adam would sit in the stump, his arms resting high on its sides. For some reason the trunk made Grandfather talk and the stump made Adam listen. It was there, on a Sunday afternoon in late October, that Adam's grandfather told him the Story of Everything.

T W O

ACTUALLY, Adam's grandfather had told him the Story long before that Sunday afternoon, but he had never told it all at once, nor had he ever finished it. Just after Adam learned to walk, in fact, Grandfather took him out to a lake and let him stand barefoot in the water. Gulls were circling overhead, and children were splashing and shrieking in the distance. Adam just stood there. A school of minnows approached, then darted away. Adam didn't notice. His toes were working the sand, but he was caught up in the shimmer of the water. After a long time, he crouched and felt the water with his hands. He didn't swirl it. He didn't splash it. He just felt it.

"Oooh!" said his grandfather, as if he were feeling the water too. He said it slowly and with a kind of reverence, all the while hanging on to Adam from behind. It was the Story's first and most important word.

Adam learned that word. He began to say it whenever he felt the wind on his face, as if it were the wind's name. He began to say it whenever he smelled a flower, as if it were the flower's name. He said it once when a car roared in the distance, and once when

4

an airplane flew low over a field. On summer evenings his grandfather would take Adam outside, fresh from a bath, and hold him
in his lap. As the sky darkened, the bone-white moon would grow
brighter and brighter. Adam would point to it and say "Oooh!"
Then he would look at his grandfather. Grandfather would wait
and wait, and then he would say "Oooh!" back. He'd say it as
soft as he could and he'd draw it out as long as he could. Before
you knew it, Adam would be asleep.

Soon there were more words, and soon the words turned into
stories. Grandfather and Adam would go to the woods and come
across a hole in the ground.

"I wonder what's down there."

"A skunk, Grandpa."

"No, I think it's a groundhog."

"Grandpa, it's a skunk."

"Maybe a rabbit."

"Grandpa, a *skunk*."

"Okay, a skunk. I wonder what its name is."

A pause. "Blackie."

"How about Stinky?"

"No, Blackie."

"But it's got a white stripe."

"*Grandpa*!"

Grandpa would give it a rest, but not for long. "What does
Blackie do down there?"

"He eats . . . stuff. Food. Garbage. From our garbage cans."

"Yummy."

"No, Grandpa, it's *not* yummy."

And so it would go. And so, after a while, it *had* to go. If you went to the woods, you had to stop at the hole. Grandpa had to wonder what was down there. Adam had to say a skunk. Grandpa had to say a groundhog.

"Skunk."

"Groundhog."

"No, Grandpa, you're supposed to say *rabbit*."

After a while, Blackie got a family. There was a mommy skunk and lots of kid skunks. There was a grandpa skunk who lived in a hole not far away. (They actually found the hole.) One night the baby of the family got lost hunting for garbage at Adam's house. Everyone went looking for him, but no one found him. Cans were falling over right and left, but the little skunk didn't come out of any of them. Nope, he was curled up and sound asleep at someone else's house, right under the porch. Before the sun came up the next day, his grandpa found him. "Right, grandpa?"

"If he had listened to his grandpa in the first place, he wouldn't have gotten lost."

And this was just one story. When you think of all the holes there are in the woods, that's a lot of stories. And when you think of everything else . . . animal tracks, for instance. If Grandfather spotted some, in mud or freshly fallen snow, he'd want to follow them. Backwards, "just for the heck of it," he'd say. The deer was going one way, but you went the other way. You wanted to know where it came from. You never did find out, but along the way you guessed. You made up a story. If you crossed a stream, Grandpa would say, "Hmm, I wonder where it came from," and soon you'd be walking upstream instead of following the tracks. And you'd be off on another story. As Adam was growing up, his grandfather was always saying, "I wonder where it came from. I wonder how it got there." He'd say it about a solitary cloud. He'd say it about a seashell in a rock. He'd say it about a freckle. He'd say it about the dumbest things. And after he said it, he'd always tell a story, though the story didn't always have an answer.

By the time he was in the second grade, Adam had figured out which of Grandfather's stories came when. There was one for when the fruit trees blossomed, and another for when the fruit was dropping to the ground. There was one for when a lamb was born, and another for when a lamb was led away to die. There was a story for when Adam was good and a story for when Adam was bad. Still, there were times, like the night a meteor streaked all the way across the sky, when Grandfather told a story that Adam had never heard before.

Whenever he heard a new story, Adam would turn it over in his head, the way he would a bird's nest that had fallen to the ground. He'd look at the top of it, then the bottom, then each and every side. Once, at school, he took apart a globe of the earth and put it back together with the South Pole on the top. He stared at it for a long, long time. He wondered what the penguins thought, being right side up for a change, and he wondered what the Eskimos thought, being upside down. And then he wondered why north was "up" and south was "down" in the first place, and where the people lived who made it that way. And after all these wonderings, he took the globe apart again and put the penguins and the Eskimos back where they belonged. He was nine at the time.

This is what Adam did with all the stories his grandfather told. He didn't know he did it, he just did it. And the stories he did it with the most were the ones about the things you couldn't see or hear or touch. The ones about the souls of trees, the things that animals knew, the two-edged ways of human beings. The ones about a Spirit.

And even though Adam heard his grandfather's stories at different times and in different places, there came that Sunday afternoon in late October when all the stories turned into one. Clouds were gathering that afternoon, and a cold wind was beginning to blow from the north. Grandfather was very insistent that Adam go to the hill, that he sit in his chair, and that he listen. Adam did, and he could practically see the stories come together, like pieces in a puzzle. Little pieces became big pieces, and big pieces became the Story. It began with Spirit.

"There was nothing else," said Grandfather. "No earth. No sun. No moon. No stars. Nothing. Only Spirit.

"And then the Spirit . . . *breathed* . . . and out they came: earth and sun, moon and stars. Hills and creeks and fields. Thunder, lightning, meteors. All in a single breath. The Spirit gave a name to what its breath had made. The name was Matter."

It was a word that Grandfather hadn't used before, at least not like that.

"And then . . . another breath . . . and fish were swimming in the creeks, and birds were flying in the air, and deer were walking on the hills. Skunks were sleeping in their holes. Things were growing. Flowers and trees. To each of them the Spirit gave a seed, its very own. To each it gave a name. And to all of them it gave the name of Life."

First Spirit, then Matter, then Life, thought Adam. He was watching how Grandfather was laying the pieces down. He had never seen him be so careful.

When all the pieces were in place, Grandfather paused. He blew sharply on his fingers, just once, and then he looked at Adam. "That's where you come in," he said. "You come from the breath of God."

Adam was ten when he heard about the breath of God, and he never forgot the moment that he did. For the rest of his life he would see his grandfather sitting on the trunk of that oak tree, about to fall as it did, telling him the Story of Everything. Adam loved the Story of Everything, and he loved his grandfather. The two were inseparable.

THREE

THEY found Adam's grandfather lying on his back at the edge of a cornfield, the dog by his side. A dusting of snow had covered him, and made him look like part of the earth. "If you gotta leave this world, that's the way to do it," neighbors said at the funeral.

Adam didn't know why you had to leave this world, and that was a piece of the Story he tried to turn over in his mind. But, hard as he tried, it wouldn't budge, and he grew weary. And then he froze inside and stayed that way till spring.

His parents could see what was happening, but they couldn't help. Adam wouldn't let them help. He performed his chores without protest. He did his homework without complaint. He got very, very good. So what could they say? How could they *get in*? Every now and then one of them would catch him staring off into space—at the dining room table, say, his schoolbooks spread out before him—and there'd be moisture in his eyes. But the moment he sensed they were there, he'd turn to his books. When he looked up, the moisture would be gone.

And so his parents waited.

That winter Adam made many trips to the skunk hole. Once, when he was scooping away some snow, he thought he heard a voice. It was either in the hole or in his head, but it was very clear. It was telling the story of Blackie, and it was coming to the end: listen to your grandfather and you won't get lost.

Adam got an idea. When spring came, he went out to the hill and sat in his carved-out chair. He looked at the trunk of the fallen oak and tried to hear the words of the Story of Everything. But all he heard was the rustle of last year's leaves, kicked up by the wind.

So Adam just sat there, fiddling with some splinters on the stump. He began to study them. Most were twisted or broken, but a few were standing upright. Adam wiggled one off and held it up to the sun. It grew warm in his fingers. His hand grew warm too, and then his arm, and then everything in him. All of a sudden he stood up from his chair and said, "I'm going to find it. I'm going to find the Story." He said it as a matter of simple fact, as if he were saying, "I'm going to get a drink of water." Then he headed home.

In spring there'd always been a story in the orchard, so the very next morning Adam went off to the orchard. The trees there were in bloom, and when Adam picked a blossom, and peeled off a petal, and held the petal up to the sun, he saw an amazing sight. Not words, but veins, delicate veins, veins transparent to light. They looked like the branches of a leafless tree. "Cool!" he whispered. Down in the well from which the petal sprang, the colors were deep and rich, purple and pink. There was moisture in that well, and from it rose dozens of stick-people, without arms or legs, huddled together with their heads bowed.

"Can we go to the library?" Adam asked his mother.

The *library*? His mother had to sit down, but they went that very evening and returned with a book. Adam pored over it. He learned that the stick-people were called stamens, that their heads were anthers, and their bodies filaments. He read about pistils and their ovaries, and he looked for them in the flowers' well. There they were! Headless people slightly swollen at their base. As the blossoms matured and their colors paled, the stick-people grew further and further apart. Adam liked it better when the blossoms were still half open, when the stick-people were standing up straight and looking every bit as if they were talking to each other.

By the time the blossoms fell, Adam was in the creek, wading toward its source, turning over stones as he sloshed along. But the Story wasn't in the creek—only bugs. "Cool!" said Adam once again. There were bugs of all kinds, tiny ones scampering for cover, and every now and then a huge one, like a centipede with claws, clinging resolutely to the bottom of a rock. Some of the rocks had tubes attached to them, little ones no longer than a fingernail. When Adam broke a tube apart, he found inside a creamy white worm, the smallest he had ever seen. How did the worm get inside the tube? he wondered. Where did it come from?

Adam couldn't ask his grandfather, so he went to the library and got another book. He discovered that the creamy worm came from an egg in the bottom of the creek; that after the worm hatched from the egg, it took little stones and glued them together on the bottom of a rock to make itself a house (that was the tube); that after a while, the worm changed into a different kind of bug, crawled out of its house, and shot up and out of the water. Then it started flying, like a moth.

"Oooh!" said Adam, not knowing why he had chosen that word. He read on. The moth-like fly was called a caddis. *Trichoptera.* Once in the air, it would fly around until it found another caddis. The two would mate. Then one of them, the female, would return to the creek, dive to the bottom, and lay her eggs there. And when an egg would hatch, out would come another white worm and build another house of stones. Grandfather never told a better story.

Each time Adam returned from the creek, or from the field, he'd have his pockets filled with rocks. He'd take them to his room and dump them in a cardboard box that he kept under his bed. At night he studied the rocks. One was flecked with black and white and something that looked like gold. Another was a smooth and uniform gray. Another contained rings that looked like they were once alive. Adam learned the names of his rocks: granite, limestone, sandstone, dolomite, quartz, shale, slate, gypsum, conglomerate.

Sometimes, when the lights were out, Adam would reach under his bed for his box and remove the rocks, one by one. He'd feel how rough they were, how smooth. He'd feel his way around their bumps and crevices. Granite, slate, sandstone: Soon he knew them in the dark. Soon he knew them in his sleep. One thing led to another, and to another, and to another, and it all began because Adam was searching for the Story of Everything.

Maybe it's in the sky, he thought on a warm summer night. So Adam snuck out of the house, lay down on the ground, and looked up at the stars. He didn't find the Story there, but he did find something else: a star that didn't flicker. Could be a planet, he thought, and he was right. Soon, with the help of a book, he found four of them: Jupiter, Saturn, Venus, and Mars.

When Adam's birthday came, his family surprised him with a telescope. Whenever the moon came out that summer, in whatever phase, Adam was out there, looking up. The moon pulled in a mysterious way at Adam's mind, and he could see it better now: craters lit and shadowed, broad dark plains, ridges, peaks, and valleys. Lines shooting like rays from a circle on the bottom. Adam brought a flashlight to his nightly observations, so he could sketch what he was seeing. During the day he added names to his sketches, the names of oceans and seas, the names of mountains and valleys, the names of craters. Latin names he got from books. Oceanus Procellarum, Mare Serenitatis, Montes Apenninus, Vallis Rheita, the craters Tycho and Clavius, and many, many more.

When there was no moon, Adam returned to the stars. He learned the constellations. He learned their names, and he learned the stories behind their names. Ursa Major, the Great Bear (the Big Dipper was little more than its tail). Back when the Bear was a human being, the story went, she was a lover of Zeus. Then Zeus's wife found out—and that's why the Bear is a bear today.

Gemini, the Twins. When one died, the other was so forlorn that Zeus reunited them forever, up in the heavens. Leo the Lion, the fiercest of them all, but no match for Hercules. He was strangled to death by the hero, the first of his twelve mighty Labors. Taurus, the Snow-White Bull, actually Zeus in disguise. A princess fell for the get-up, climbed on his back, and let him swim her off to Crete. Orion, the Hunter, mistakenly killed by a virgin goddess. When the goddess couldn't revive him, she lifted him up to the sky, far from the dangerous Scorpion. Pegasus, the Winged Horse, sprung up from blood, stung by a gadfly, forever ridden by a boy (Adam made that part up) on the slopes of Mount Olympus.

Adam liked the stories as much as the stars, which meant he learned a lot of stories that summer. But of all the stories that he learned, none was the one that he was looking for. None was the Story of Everything.

In fact, no matter where Adam looked that year—orchard, creek, field, or sky—he never did find the Story of Everything. He found a lot of other things, however, things that helped him forget what he had lost. So before the year was out, he took the sadness in his heart, carried it to a distant region of his mind, and laid it in a secret place. He didn't bury it. He just covered it, as though with branches of pine. And then he turned his back and walked away. All he kept was a picture of a carved-out stump and an October day and a grandfather telling him the Story of Everything. That was the moment he had loved, the moment when it all came together, if only for an afternoon.

FOUR

THE friends who had climbed with Adam over the fallen oak tree stayed away during the summer that he searched for the Story of Everything. Once school started, however, they were back together again, and not too many summers after that, they were sneaking beer and cigarettes out to a hidden ledge at an abandoned limestone quarry. There, on sultry summer evenings, they would swim in the quarry's deep blue water, and talk late into the night about basketball, cars, music, and girls.

They talked about school too. Adam's friends knew that he was smart. They knew, in fact, that he was very smart. But there were things about him that they didn't know. They didn't know how hard he had looked for the Story of Everything, or what he had found instead. They didn't know about the trips he kept taking to the library, or the rocks that were under his bed, or the sketches he kept even now in a drawer.

Nor did they know about the patterns.

The ones in Adam's head, I mean. They were coming out now, constellations of a different kind. Some were simple structures. Some were complex systems. It's hard to explain, but some of them were "pure" patterns, constellations devoid of stars. When one "appeared," Adam would simply connect the dots . . . without the dots. Then he'd look the pattern over the way he would a story—top, bottom, each and every side.

Every now and then Adam's friends would catch a glimpse of what was going on inside his head. It usually happened at the quarry, as darkness was setting in and waves were lapping quietly at the limestone ledge. Adam would start to puzzle—about God, about sex, about an ant that happened to be crawling up his arm. About anything. The darker it got, the more he puzzled. He'd puzzle this way, and then he'd puzzle that way. His friends would listen for a while, and then they'd say, "Yeah, right," and turn the conversation back to basketball, cars, music, and girls. Adam, they said, was "out there."

Adam didn't mind being "out there," but he wanted to find someone else who was. So he turned again to books. He read about a time when people thought the earth was flat. If you dug into it, they believed, you would dig forever. Later, they discovered that the earth was round. A churchman came along who studied astronomy and mathematics in his spare time. His name was Copernicus, and, said the books, he was *way* out there. He shocked the world by saying the earth went around the sun.

"Shocked the world?" said Adam when he read that. "Shocked?" Then, of course, he realized that in the time of Copernicus most everyone believed the opposite: that the earth was the center of the universe, and that the sun went around it.

They believed it passionately, as if it were a truth from God. "The scorn which I had to fear on account of the newness and absurdity of my opinion," Copernicus wrote, "almost drove me to abandon a work already undertaken." Adam didn't understand that fear, but because of it, Copernicus spent years checking and rechecking his calculations. He didn't publish his idea until he reached the point where he didn't care anymore what people thought. He was on his deathbed.

It took Copernicus an entire lifetime to make the change, Adam thought, but how simple it was! Copernicus picked up a stick and turned it around. He put the sun where the earth was and the earth where the sun was. Then everything else fell into place—all the movements of the sun and moon, all the movements of the stars and planets.

Adam followed the story of Copernicus all the way to Galileo. He read how Galileo made a telescope (he called it a "spy-glass") and pointed it up at the heavens. Now he could see what Copernicus never did. He saw stars by the thousands, ten times the number that anyone had known about. He saw spots on the sun, dark ones. No one had known about them either. Galileo saw the very same planets that Adam had. He saw moons going around Jupiter, not one of them but four. He saw something that looked like handles on Saturn, one on either side. Maybe they were moons, he wrote. (They were actually rings, but Galileo's telescope wasn't strong enough to tell.) No one had ever seen these things before. No one had even imagined them.

Awesome! thought Adam as he read. He would have loved being there—in Italy, in 1609, caught up with the whole city of Venice in the excitement of the telescope. He would have loved being at the center of the excitement. He would have loved being Galileo.

We lived at different times, Adam reckoned, and we lived in different places. But we lived on the very same earth and we observed the very same moon. Eliminate a few centuries and we could have been standing side by side. I could have used his spyglass. We could have compared notes.

Adam's reckonings were not that far-fetched. He and Galileo could well have been standing side by side because they saw the very same mountains and the very same valleys on the moon. They saw the very same plains and craters and streaks of white. They both made sketches of what they saw, Adam with a pencil, Galileo with watercolors. Adam studied maps of the moon; Galileo had been the first to publish them. "It is a most beautiful and delightful sight to behold the body of the moon," Galileo wrote in his book, *The Starry Messenger*. Adam remembered the words as if he had heard them in person.

Had he lived in Galileo's time, Adam went on to think, he could have talked to him about the strange idea of this fellow Copernicus. He could have watched with Galileo as Venus went through its phases, and he could have concluded with him that Copernicus was right. The logic was clear. When Venus was at its smallest in the sky, it was also fully lit. That meant it was far away from the earth, on the opposite side of the sun, and that the earth was seeing its sunny side. When Venus got bigger, it was only half lit. That's because it was approaching the earth, and the earth was seeing more of its dark side. And when Venus was at its largest, it looked in the telescope like a tiny crescent moon. That meant it was on the same side of the sun as the earth, and that the earth was seeing almost all of its dark side. The phases of Venus meant Venus was going around the sun.

If only, sometime in his life, he could make a discovery like that! thought Adam. Moons orbiting the planets and the planets orbiting the sun, the bodies closer to their hub getting around faster. No wonder Galileo gave "infinite thanks to God" for making him "the first observer of marvels kept hidden in obscurity for all previous centuries."

There was another tale that Adam read. It involved a man who lived in England two-and-a-half centuries after Galileo, in the 1800s. He was a collector, just like Adam, only he collected beetles. "I will give proof of my zeal," the man wrote. "One day, on tearing off some old bark, I saw two rare beetles, and seized one in each hand; then I saw a third and new kind, which I could not bear to lose, so that I popped the one which I held in my right hand into my mouth."

Adam gasped. Before he could go on reading, he had to get up, pour himself a glass of water, and rinse out his mouth.

The man who put the bug in his mouth was Charles Darwin, and his curiosity about nature eventually got him a job aboard a ship called the *Beagle*. The *Beagle* left England in 1831 to survey the coast of South America down to its tip and back up the other side. Darwin was only twenty-two when he set sail, just a few years older than Adam. His job was to study the lay of the land. And study it he did, on a journey that circled the globe and kept him seasick for five years. Darwin saw how volcanoes and earthquakes had shaped the structure of coastlines, uplifting some areas and depressing others, in one case carrying fossils from the sea to a height of twelve thousand feet. He saw patterns in coral reefs, in particular how they were formed by the skeletons of tiny creatures that had died.

But the most important pattern that Darwin found was that in the beaks of little birds. The *Beagle* had landed on some volcanic islands off the coast of Ecuador. Darwin was fascinated by the variety of tortoises and lizards that lived there. By the variety of birds, too, especially the little finches. Darwin saw that finches with powerful beaks ate large seeds, that finches with weaker beaks ate little seeds, and that finches with delicate beaks didn't eat seeds at all. They ate insects. Each kind of finch, each species, had a beak suited to the food that was available in its whereabouts. It was an intriguing pattern, and Darwin thought about it all the way home to England. How did it come about?

While Darwin continued to ponder that question, another Englishman set out for South America. His name was Alfred Wallace, and he wanted to sail up the Amazon River to collect animals that Europeans had never seen. A thousand miles up the river, he turned up a tributary, the Rio Negro. It was swollen with rain, so he and his guides found themselves paddling over land, sometimes at tree level. Wallace found forty kinds of butterfly that no European had known of. He found a different species of alligator, a caiman, "which I skinned and stuffed, much to the amusement of the Indians." Grandfather had been right about what you could find by going upstream.

After four years of exploration, Wallace decided to head back to England. He started back down the Rio Negro with a hundred live animals, but by the time he reached the Amazon, two-thirds of them had died. Three weeks later his ship caught fire, and he watched from a lifeboat as his entire collection was lost. "I had not one specimen to illustrate the unknown lands I had trod," he wrote. Adam, a collector himself, knew how bad he must have felt.

But Wallace was not deterred. After returning to England, he sailed all the way to Malaysia. He wanted to collect specimens from a different part of the world. Had any man seen such a variety of life? Adam asked himself. Wallace wondered how all the species had originated.

One night, on a small island between New Guinea and Borneo, Wallace lay sick with fever, when "suddenly there flashed upon me the idea of the survival of the fittest." And to whom did he write about that idea? To Charles Darwin. "I never saw a more striking coincidence," said Darwin when he got the letter, for he himself had hit upon the same idea some twenty years before. Like Copernicus, however, he had been hesitant to publish it. But now two men had seen the same pattern in nature. "All species have changed," Darwin wrote, "and are still slowly changing." That was the key. Species were *evolving*, one into another, through a process called "natural" selection. Why can't nature do what mankind does already? Darwin asked. He was thinking of breeders of animals and cultivators of plants. "Why, if man can by patience select variation most useful to himself, should nature fail in selecting variation useful, under changing conditions of life, to her living products?" Adam knew all about the selection that breeders and cultivators did. If you lived on a farm, you had to know. So "natural" selection seemed perfectly natural to him. He could believe there was a pattern to it, hidden though it was in eons of time.

Adam got lost in the stories of Darwin and Wallace. He crossed oceans with them, and sailed down coastlines, and went up rivers, and took off for distant islands. He paddled silently among the trees of swollen rain forests. He took a closer look at the lay of his own land, at the hills behind the barn, at the tiny caves, at the birds (he learned which ones were finches). He drew, he read his heroes' notes, he made his own. He wanted to find the patterns.

The men that Adam read about became as real to him as his friends at the quarry. In their lifetimes, they had been out there—and up there and down there and over there. Adam wanted to go there too. But he didn't know how, he didn't know where, and he didn't know when. And that is why he kept going back to the quarry on summer nights, and why he kept listening to his friends talk about basketball, and cars, and music, and girls.

FIVE

ONE evening after dinner, Adam hopped in the family pickup and went off on a long drive to nowhere in particular. There were details in the stories of Galileo and Darwin that he didn't understand, and they were bothering him. It wasn't a night for the quarry. It was a night to be alone and think.

"A bumpy moon," Adam was saying as his truck bounced along a gravel road, kicking up a long trail of dust. "A sun with spots. So what?"

He was thinking about Galileo. Authorities had been furious when Galileo's telescope revealed that there were mountains and craters on the moon, and spots on the sun. Didn't Galileo know that the moon was "supposed" to be smooth? That the sun was "supposed" to be unblemished? That all the heavens, in fact, were "supposed" to be perfect and pure?

"Says who?" Adam had said. When he looked into the matter, he discovered that the who was Aristotle. Though Aristotle had lived almost two thousand years before Galileo, his authority had been immense. It had woven itself into the authority of a church on the lookout for heretics. And that church had claimed that Galileo had sullied the heavens. Not only that, he had agreed with Copernicus, in opposition to Aristotle, that the earth circled the sun. That puts you at odds with the Bible, said the church. No, it doesn't, said Galileo, not if you really understand the Bible. The church didn't care how Galileo understood the Bible. He was put on trial and threatened with torture, fully aware that another man, a monk in fact, had been burned at the stake for saying what he was saying.

That's what Adam didn't understand. If Aristotle had been alive in 1609 (Adam was sure of it) he would have looked in Galileo's telescope and changed his mind. So would the writers of the Bible. So why wouldn't the church? Why would the church go to such extremes, torturing and killing in the Bible's name?

Nor did Adam understand what happened in the aftermath of Darwin. No one was tortured or killed in his day, but there was plenty of condemnation. Churchmen condemned the scientists: *God* made the creatures of the earth, not natural selection. God made the species just as they are, and gave them names that would last forever. He made human beings just as they are, and placed them at the top of creation. Life was created just as it is. There wasn't time for it to evolve.

The scientists hit back, harder than in Galileo's day: The creation story is nothing but myth, they said. The making of separate species is myth. The creation of human beings is myth. The Bible itself is myth. Its timeline cannot be correct.

And on the accusations went, back and forth.

What Adam didn't understand this time was why it had to be one or the other, why it had to be creation *or* evolution. Why couldn't creation evolve? he asked himself over and over. It seemed so obvious, so simple. It's what Darwin himself had said, right at the end of *The Origin of Species*. The Creator had "breathed" life into a few original forms.

As Adam drove on that evening, he began to suspect that something else must have been going on in the days of Galileo and Darwin. There must have been another hand in the pot, stirring things up. And the hand, he suspected, belonged to someone (I should say some*thing*) he hadn't thought about in a while. It belonged to the Story of Everything.

It was the words people had used. Words like *God* and *heavens* and *earth*. Words like *life* and *origins*, *purpose* and *pure*. Words about the *names* of creatures and the *place* of human beings. These were words that Adam's grandfather had used.

But his grandfather had never said "torture" or "killing." He had never said "condemnation." Maybe he hadn't known about these things. Maybe he'd known but didn't want to say. Adam's suspicions grew. He looked at the moon, which was just now rising full and golden. It dawned on him, for the very first time: What you see is always the same. The moon doesn't rotate, like the earth. It doesn't spin. You never see its other side. And then he thought: the Story doesn't rotate either. It has a side you never see.

By the time Adam got home, his suspicions had turned into anger. He had once loved the Story of Everything, but it deserted him when he needed it the most. Good riddance, he now thought. Adam struggled in his sleep that night, and in his dreams he searched once again for the Story. He never found it. When he awoke in the morning, the Story of Everything seemed alien to him. I no longer know it, he said. I no longer know what kind of story it is.

SIX

ON the night of Adam's bumpy ride, the Story of Everything was where it had been for years, sitting at home in its library, in the comfort of its favorite chair. It had no idea where Adam was, or what he was doing, or how angry he had gotten. It had, in fact, forgotten all about Adam. It had forgotten a lot of other things as well, like most of its existence. But that's the way it is with stories. They come, they go. They remember, they forget. They lose their way, they find it again. Just like people.

The library in which the Story of Everything was sitting was, to put it mildly, unusual. It contained books of every size and shape—tall and short, thick and thin, some freshly shelved, some covered with centuries of dust. New arrivals were piling up in the corners, wherever there was room. The books were written in different languages, but all of them told the same story, the Story of Everything. These books said "always" to the Story of Everything, as in, "You always were and you always will be." They were like a thousand mirrors, and the library was like a sanctuary.

On this particular evening, the eyes of the Story of Everything lingered on the oldest of these books, a massive volume lying on its side in a glass case, under lock and key. Its leather cover was scuffed and worn, its title rubbed away. Although the Story of Everything didn't remember many things about his life, he did remember the birth of that book. And though the incident had taken place more than five hundred years before, to the Story of Everything it seemed like yesterday. Closing his eyes, he could still smell the ink lying in wait on rows and rows of metal type, could feel the paper gently blanket him, could hear the great screw twisting down, and then, after the compressing and the lifting (he nearly lost his breath), could see . . . himself, as though he were outside his body, looking down.

The Story of Everything thought he was remembering his birth, but it was only his birth in print. He was the first story ever to be printed, the first to become a book like the one you are holding in your hands.

What a moment that was! One copy came off the press and was stitched together, then another and another. Covers were glued on. All of a sudden there were tens and hundreds of books. At first, the Story of Everything tried to keep track of each and every one. He followed one into a great hall, where he heard himself being read aloud, the words echoing like thunder off walls of stone. He followed another onto a table, where the words came out in quiet murmurs. He tracked a third onto a lap, and there he felt himself being taken in without sound, the lips of his reader barely moving. It was a strange silence, and for some reason the Story of Everything found it disturbing. He couldn't tell what his silent reader was making of him; and yet, once he was in that reader, and not just in print, he had a strange and fleeting sense of being home again.

How things have changed, the Story now thought, scanning the shelves that surrounded him. He had loved the printing press. Not the act itself of reproduction—there was no pleasure in it— but what resulted from it. All those clones. All the people they attracted. All the words the people said. "Unerring." "Infallible." "Absolute." "Written by God Himself." The Story of Everything loved being the first book. He loved being the only book. It never occurred to him that other books might follow, or say that he was wrong.

SEVEN

WHAT a shock it had been, then, when the Story of Everything discovered, in the time of Copernicus and Galileo, that other books were indeed being printed, and when he heard that some of them were saying, though not to his face, that he *was* wrong. He was wrong about the earth and where it stood, wrong about the sun and moon and how they moved about.

Adam had read about the very incident. What Adam hadn't read, however—what history hadn't recorded—was that the Story of Everything had asked to speak to the other books. Actually, his "asking" was more like a summons.

The earth didn't "stand" anywhere, the new books said when they arrived. It was out in space. There was nothing for it to stand "on."

How odd, thought the Story of Everything.

"The earth is a sphere," they said. "It moves through space. It spins."

Ridiculous, thought the Story.

"And the sun . . . it doesn't rise. It doesn't fall. It stands still."

31

"Impossible," muttered the Story. He was getting red in the face.

Then came the shocker. "The sun, not the earth, is at the center of things. We are outsiders looking in."

"Never!" shouted the Story of Everything, bolting up. "Never!"

The other books cowered, but they wouldn't stop. "The moon has crags and craters, pits and jagged edges!"

"No!" shouted the Story. "It is perfectly smooth."

"The sun has spots."

"Baloney!"

"Take a look," they said. "Look in the telescope!"

The Story of Everything refused.

"Here! Look at Jupiter!" they shouted. "Look at all its moons!"

"There is only one moon!" yelled the Story of Everything.

"Look! Look in the telescope! There's more to Everything than you think."

And the Story whose name was Everything refused. He turned his back and walked away.

What happened in the aftermath of that incident still troubled the Story of Everything. In no time at all, the people who loved him fell silent. But those who worshiped him did not. They became vociferous. They were filled with rage. They forbad the reading of the new books. They interrogated the people who wrote them. They put the writers in prison. Some of them they tortured. Some they tied to the stake and burned.

The Story of Everything didn't condone these activities, but neither did he do a thing to stop them. And to this day that bothered him. Not all of those who fought for him acted like criminals, he told himself. Only a few actually killed. Still, he had stood by and let it happen. He had even drawn from it a silent, guilty satisfaction.

What disturbed the Story the most, however, was not the fact that he had been wrong, or that he had closed his eyes and washed his hands of evil. It was something that had happened even before Galileo made his spyglass. A star, never before seen, flared up in the sky. People thought the star was being born, even though in actuality it was dying. When the Story of Everything heard about that birth, he panicked. For birth in the heavens meant death in the heavens, a going out of being as well as a coming in. If stars, eternal stars, could come and go, he had thought, why not stories? And why not a Story of Everything?

EIGHT

I T took about a century for the Story of Everything to learn from his mistake with the new books. Even now he could remember the day he apologized and asked if he might, after all, look in their telescope. Once he took his first look, he couldn't turn away. He stayed up all night. He wasn't surprised by what he saw, but he was humbled nevertheless. The new books were right: there was a lot to Everything, a lot more than he had realized. And there was a lot to what they were calling "science."

When morning came, the Story of Everything said something strange, more to himself than to anyone else. I'm still alive, he mumbled. I was wrong, but I'm still alive. It was a stunning revelation.

In an instant, another followed: maybe a Story of Everything doesn't have to get everything right.

These revelations were reassuring to the Story of Everything. He was calmer, therefore, and even a little playful, when another set of books gathered around him some two hundred years after Galileo. They all bore the name *Evolution*, but they were far from being of one mind.

The Story of Everything remembered how menacing they had seemed. "What's the problem?" he asked.

This group was bolder than the previous one, more like a mob. "You're wrong again," they shouted to his face.

Several of them began taking bones out of sacks they had brought. Some of the bones were intact. Others were nothing more than fragments. The other books laid the bones out in a row, from the oldest on the left to the newest on the right.

"Look at these bones," they said.

This time the Story of Everything looked. He looked at the skeletons formed by the bones, and the skulls in particular. Well, he thought, there *is* a pattern.

"You said that human beings came from God," one of the books said. "But look, they came from the apes."

Could it be? thought the Story.

"You were wrong about the creatures, too," said another. "You said they stay the same. But they don't. They change. They get more complex."

How was I supposed to know? thought the Story of Everything. A plan was taking shape in his mind: he would negotiate.

"You put human beings at the top!" a third book charged. "But they're only one of a thousand branches."

They belong at the top, thought the Story of Everything. Besides, they loved it when I put them there. But he remembered that he had erred when he put the earth at the center of the universe.

Once the first accusations were made, others followed. Some were contradictory, but none were too trivial to bring up.

"You skipped the beginning."

"You got the beginning wrong."

"There was no creation."

"You got the creation wrong."

"The plot is off."

"The trouble is, you've got a plot."

Design. Chance. Purpose. Accident. First Cause. Final Cause. Increasing complexity. Irreducible complexity. Survival of the good. Survival of the fittest. God. No God. They used a lot of big words and they asked a lot of long questions. After a while the Story of Everything lost track of what they were saying.

Finally, a conciliatory voice spoke up. "You're not a Story of Everything," it began gently, as if breaking some bad news. "You're really a Story of Spirit, and evolution is a Story of Life. We're talking about two different things."

A number of nods and murmurs of approval followed. There was even one resounding "Amen."

"You are religion, not science."

More Amens.

But then the loudest and the angriest voice of the day yelled from the rear, "You're dead!"

In the awkward hush that followed, the Story of Everything gathered his thoughts. "A few distinctions are in order," he began.

"Perhaps I am a Story of Spirit and not a Story of Life, and not even a Story of Everything. Perhaps I am religion and not science. But I would ask you to read me very carefully. Because if you do, you will see that when I say something, I mean it. When I say *this*, I mean *this* and not *that*. Except of course where *this* means *that* and not the other thing."

Throwing up a cloud of smoke was new to the Story of Everything, and his own head began to get a little foggy, but he kept on going. "You will also see that when I say *that*, I mean *that*, not *this*, regardless of the other thing." That's better, he thought, and he went on to cover all the permutations of *this* and *that* and the other thing. He got so good at making distinctions that he even threw in a couple of footnotes.

The confrontation didn't end after his response, but everyone was so confused they thought it had. They began to look at their watches, and in no time at all they had called it quits.

The Story of Everything had breathed a great sigh of relief after this second incident. He had never done the *this*-and-the-*that* thing before, much less the *this*-and-the-*that*-and-the-other-thing thing, and it had come off rather well. His followers, however, were furious, and those who worshiped him were the angriest of all. They didn't kill their enemies this time, but they did put some of them on trial. None were imprisoned and none were tortured, but skirmishes continued to flare up. Laws were passed and revoked, then passed and revoked again. But the Story of Everything stayed above the fray.

By the time Adam came along, the Story had learned a lot about his followers, at least about the ones who worshiped him. They don't know me, he kept on saying to himself. I don't think they love me either. What they do love is their own certainty.

Later, he reached another conclusion: I may not know myself that well.

And that is why the Story of Everything was spending so much time these days in his library, trying to remember, trying to get to know himself, trying to find his way. He really wasn't happy being a Story of Spirit, or whatever the *Evolution* books had said he was. He wasn't happy making distinctions. Stories of Everything don't make distinctions, he said to himself. They don't separate. They integrate.

He reflected more deeply: I've given up parts of myself. Maybe I'll always exist, but as what? A Story of a Couple of Things? A Story of Just One Thing? I am a Story of Everything, he insisted. But he had no idea anymore of how to be one.

NINE

WHEN Adam went away to college, he left his friends behind—not just the ones at the quarry, but the ones in the books. He left his dreams behind too, and his hopes of going "out there." He had a job to do. He had to learn practical things about soil and seeds and livestock and weather and anything else that would enable him to carry on his family's way of life.

An incident in his second year, however, changed all that. It started with a report that Adam wrote early in the fall semester. Everything about the report was perfect: the references, the method, the observations, the calculations, the analysis. But it was so concise, so brief. Only two-and-a-half pages.

"Why not add some interpretation?" the teacher wrote on the last page. "Speculate a bit." And that started a conversation one morning after class that carried through lunch and well into the afternoon. It went from the lecture hall to the cafeteria to a bench in a park off campus. The report was soon forgotten, for the teacher had discovered in Adam a mind that was not concise at all. It was reaching for something grand. It was struggling with its own uniqueness. What is this young man doing in a school of agriculture? the teacher asked herself.

It was the kind of autumn day when everyone wanted to be outside, flying a kite or throwing a football or just going for a walk. The bench on which Adam and his teacher were sitting faced a river whose surface was as smooth as glass. Leaves of yellow, orange, maroon, and brown drifted down like huge snowflakes and landed on the water with hardly a splash—in places, it seemed, of their own choosing. Slowly they went on their way to wherever—the only hint that the river was moving. And as they left, others drifted down, caught a flash of sunlight, and replaced them.

Something was released in Adam on that occasion, and he let his teacher see it. He talked for hours. The midday sun, which had warmed him, gave way to clouds and an occasional chill. As the wind picked up, leaves began to skitter across the grass. One of them got caught at the base of the bench and began to whistle softly.

By the end of that afternoon, Adam's teacher was seeing in him things she had seen in no other student. A freshness, an urgency, a facility with the structures of thought. She saw something else as well—a place of sadness and anger. She saw a longing, too, saw it more than Adam did, and so she said to him, "You are meant for something else." She said he had a gift.

In the days that followed, Adam thought about his teacher's words, and as he did, a strange feeling came over him. It was like a voice that said, "You're different." Adam never knew he had a gift because he assumed that the students sitting next to him thought the way that he did. Now he learned that they did not. He learned that he had received something, and that he had a choice: he could open up the gift or not.

During the rest of that year, Adam walked around campus more slowly. He sat in the back of lecture halls so he could see the other students as well as the teachers. His mind drifted. He thought of his grandfather following animal trails the way no one else had. He thought about the rocks that were still under his bed at home. He thought about Venice in 1609 and the *Beagle* in 1831. He thought about the pattern that Galileo found, and the one that Darwin did—one in the immensity of space, the other in the immensity of time.

By spring Adam had decided to leave the study of agriculture and concentrate on the study of life. On biology in particular. Two scientists, James Watson and Francis Crick, had just announced that they had discovered the structure of genetic material. They described the structure as a double helix and said it was shaped like a spiral staircase. It was a pattern that Adam had once seen in his mind, only it had looked to him like a twisting, diving roller coaster track. But it was all track and no roller coaster, so Adam paid it little attention.

When that structure turned out to be the key to life, however, Adam couldn't believe it. Watson and Crick, he concluded, were modern-day equivalents of Copernicus and Galileo, of Darwin and Wallace. It was still possible, he realized, to discover in nature a pattern that no one else had seen before. Adam decided then and there to spend his life looking for one. Practicality went out the window: Adam's dreams were back.

T E N

S O Adam pursued his dreams. After finishing college, he went on to graduate school, this time to learn all that he could about the amazing structure that lay at the heart of life. The double helix had billions of steps in its staircase, billions of *a*'s, *c*'s, *g*'s, and *t*'s. Each meant something. Each did something. Adam wanted to find out what. He wanted to crack the genetic code.

But the code was complex, and the staircase was long, and you had to take one step at a time. It didn't matter. Adam enjoyed the laboratory, and he enjoyed the bar where he talked late into the night with his teachers and fellow students. After a few years, he was publishing small notes that added this detail and that to the Story of Life. (That's what he called it: the Story of Life.) He was happy where he was, and he wasn't in a hurry to do anything else. And so time passed.

One afternoon, as Adam's schooling was drawing to a close, a young woman asked him out to coffee. Her name was Elise, and she lived in an apartment two doors down the hall from his. They spent most of that afternoon talking, and soon they began to see more of each other. It turned out that Elise was a part-time student and a full-time activist. Over the course of a summer Adam eased up on his lab work, and Elise snuck out of meetings so they could spend more time together. They would go to a beach and rent a boat, and she would teach him how to sail. On weekends they went off to wilderness areas, each trip longer and more demanding than the last. They recuperated together in her apartment, indulging in the pleasure of little things—a decent meal, a favorite television program—while loads of laundry were cycling through machines in the basement.

At first Elise had been attracted by Adam's intelligence, by the sheer speed of his intuition. But as she got to know him, she discovered something else. Adam possessed an innocence that she had never seen before. It was a wounded innocence, to be sure; it had survived something. To an idealist like Elise, it was a powerful magnet, and it drew her close to him.

For his part, Adam admired Elise's confidence. She knew her way around, and she had been around. But then she had come from a family who knew their way around, and who had also been around. When the two of them began to make love, Adam was like a boy. He never tired of looking at Elise, never tired of touching her. And when he entered her for the first time (it was his first time with any woman) the oddest thing happened. It seemed to Adam that he was standing knee-deep in water, lost in its never-ending shimmer. It seemed that he was staring at a perfect moon, feeling a cool and wondrous clarity. It seemed that he had been in this place before.

In the fall Adam took Elise to his childhood home. He showed her the barn, the creek, the fruit trees, the sandstone rocks with their seashells. He took her out to the quarry where he and his friends once swam. All the while he told her stories from his growing up, the little ones but not the big one. In fact, when he took her to the hill where the oak once stood, he hardly said a word. She didn't notice the remains of the carved-out stump.

Adam graduated that December. Snow was falling on the day he did, laying a seal on the year just past. In the evening Adam told Elise of a decision he had made: to turn down an offer to do research elsewhere, to accept an offer to stay where he was. He was twenty-eight. He wanted to be with her.

ELEVEN

THE following spring Elise told Adam that she hadn't been feeling well, that she had been to the doctor, and that she was pregnant.

She had saved the announcement for a Sunday morning. They were at one of their favorite places, a small diner with cloths of red and white covering the tables. It was May, and the first Sunday of the year in which tables were set up outside. Elise waited until they had finished eating and were relaxing over a cup of coffee.

"Are you sure?" Adam asked.

"Yes," she said.

The waitress brought the check. Elise paid, Adam left a tip, and they walked in silence back to their apartment building. At the entrance Adam said, "I need to go for a walk." His tone said, I need to go alone.

Adam took his solitary walk, and then he returned to Elise's apartment and asked her to join him. They walked together, on and off, for most of the afternoon. By evening they understood that each of them wanted the child Elise was carrying. They also understood that each was unsure about getting married. So they decided simply to move in together and see what happened.

The first thing that happened was Elise's attempt to learn more about Adam's work. She was away a lot, and when she was home, Adam was often "away" too—in a world of his own.

"I've never been to your lab," she said to him one morning. "I'd like to see what you do."

Adam obliged. He walked Elise over to a massive building, took her upstairs, and opened the gray metal door to his laboratory. They chatted with some technicians, and Adam explained what various pieces of equipment were for. He told her what his research group was trying to find out, and what he in particular was looking for. Much of it seemed obscure to Elise, and tedious, and removed from life. She couldn't help but realize that Adam's world really *was* different from her own.

At lunch Elise said, "There's a meeting a week from tonight. I'd like to show you what I do."

Adam went to that meeting, and when Elise asked him to help out at a rally, he agreed. He passed out flyers for a while, and then he just watched. When Elise got up to speak, he saw the gifts she had. He felt guilty: Elise was doing remarkable things, and he knew he should be more involved in them. But he also knew, deeper down, that he would never be. Adam went to a few more meetings after that; he helped out at a few more rallies; but that was it.

Elise gave birth to a son the following winter. They named him James, but from the beginning they called him Jamie. It didn't take long for them to work out a rhythm of care and work. And separation. Adam would go to the lab in the morning and return in the afternoon. Then Elise would leave and return at night, sometimes very late. Every now and then, one of them took the baby along. In the first year of his life, Jamie saw a lot of his parents, and a lot of their two different worlds. But his parents saw little of each other.

TWELVE

WHEN Jamie began to walk, an urge arose in Adam, a compelling urge, and it surprised him. He couldn't explain why, but he had to get his son to water. Not just *to* water, but *into* water. Barefoot, so his toes could feel the sand while his hands touched the coolness and his eyes took in the shimmer. It was beyond question: these were things that Jamie should know.

When the weather finally turned warm, Adam took Jamie to the lake where Elise had taught him to sail. Seagulls were fighting on the beach when they arrived. Jamie ran right at them. He saw children splashing in the shallows. He went after them too, straight into the water. He fell over once and then a second time. Each time Adam picked him up, each time Jamie sputtered, and each time he kept on going. Adam grabbed him by the hand and pointed out a school of minnows skirting the shoreline. He held Jamie still so they would come closer. But Jamie had other ideas.

It wasn't long before the children who were playing in the shallows had taught Jamie how to smack the water with his hands. They led him ashore, sat him on the beach, and gave him a shovel and pail. Jamie threw sand to the wind, and the children darted away, squealing and shrieking and egging him on. Half of what he threw landed in his own face, but it didn't seem to matter. Watching from close by, Adam had to smile. He admired his son's abandon, but it wasn't the baptism he had had in mind.

Adam and Jamie stayed at the beach until the sun went down. Adam delayed their departure because he wanted to see how a bank of dark clouds, which was about to cover the setting sun, would look against an orange sky. Jamie grew restless in his father's arms, but once he was in the car he fell instantly asleep, lulled by the sound of rain on the roof and the rhythmic drumming of the windshield wipers. The rain was heavy, and Adam had to concentrate on the pair of red lights in front of him. But the squall passed quickly.

Adam could then relax and let his thoughts wander. By the time he reached the expressway, they had taken a surprising turn. How, he wondered, had he ended up in this car with this child? This child whose nature seemed so different from his own?

"Where were you?" a worried Elise asked when they finally got home. Adam was slow to answer because his thoughts had taken yet another turn. When Elise had opened the door, they had said: here is someone else whose nature is very different from my own.

It was a moment of truth, and in that moment a second urge arose in Adam, as compelling as the first. He had to tell Elise about his grandfather's Story. So the next morning he took a chance and spoke about the storm and the tree and the carved-out stump and all that had happened on the hill. He told her how he had searched for the Story and never found it. Adam couldn't believe he was telling Elise these things because he thought he had left them behind.

Elise listened as well as she could, but there was a lot going on in the world, and there was a lot that needed to be done, and besides, there was a baby waking up in the next room. When Adam was done, she said, more honestly than she had wished, "It's only a Story of Everything."

THIRTEEN

STORIES that are trying to find their way often lose a lot of sleep, and the Story of Everything was no exception. Nearly every night his rest was being disturbed by dreams of bones, bones that danced out of sacks and lay themselves in perfect order on the floor. Bones by the hundreds, and all in that irritatingly perfect order. In the middle of one such dream, a thought occurred to the Story of Everything. It was a frightening thought, an unthinkable thought. The thought was (you may have guessed), Could *I* have evolved?

Hard as he tried the next morning, the Story of Everything could not *remember* evolving, but how could he tell for sure? I'll lay out some books, he decided. I'll lay out some books like the bones in my dreams.

That very afternoon the Story skipped his nap, headed straight for the library, and cleared the large worktable that filled an alcove off to the side. He unlocked the glass case that contained the oldest of his books. He lifted the book up out of the case and laid it, reverentially, on a corner of the table. Then he approached a wall of shelves, closed his eyes (he was trying to be random), and retrieved a second book. He crossed the room, closed his eyes again, and got a third. He kept on selecting books like that, some from high up on the shelves, some from down low, always with his eyes closed. A couple dozen ought to do it, he said to himself, but then, just to be sure, he added a few more to the pile that was building up on the table.

Now the Story of Everything arranged the books in the order of their age. After the oldest came several more from the fifteenth century, then others from the sixteenth, the seventeenth, the eighteenth, the nineteenth, and the twentieth. The rows formed from left to right, one beneath the other.

My whole life, said the Story, looking over the table. My whole life right before my eyes. But the Story of Everything was mistaken. What lay on the table wasn't his whole life at all, but only his life in print.

Looking at the books, the Story of Everything saw indeed that some things had changed. The new books were smaller than the older ones. They were written in more languages. The print inside was finer. The individual letters were different too. They were stiffer now—straight, sharp, and angular. They looked like little blocks. Funny, thought the Story of Everything, I like them that way. He liked the E's, F's, H's, and T's, but not the snaky C's and S's. He was a straight story, after all. He was orthodox.

Now the Story of Everything closed his eyes again, felt for the oldest of his books, and opened it to a passage at random. He opened all the other books to the very same passage. He smoothed the pages down and read what lay before him. He took his time doing it, and when he was done, he had his answer: no matter how the passages looked, no matter what their language, they were all the same.

I have *not* evolved, the Story concluded. I'm nothing like the bones.

Satisfied with his conclusion, yet strangely disappointed, the Story of Everything began closing the books and returning them to their shelves. When he came to the last (it was the oldest), he began to feel nostalgic. He sat down and ran his hand over the open pages. He touched the words one by one. They seemed to flow in an odd way from the very tip of his finger. Suddenly an image came to the Story of Everything. He saw ink flowing from a pen. He saw a huddled figure dipping the pen into a small pot and copying words from one page to another. The figure was . . . writing.

Writing?

"Oh my God!" the Story whispered. He remembered the attic.

FOURTEEN

SPECIFICALLY, the Story remembered a trunk in the attic, and soon he was climbing a narrow flight of stairs and opening the attic door. He started looking for the trunk of his memory, pushing aside wardrobes and chairs and lamps and old musical instruments, sweating and coughing from all the dust he was stirring up. Once he had opened a window at either end of the attic, he began to breathe more easily. He also had better light, so it wasn't long before he came upon what he was looking for.

It opened easily.

"Look at this!" he said under his breath.

Inside the trunk were clumps of pages that looked like they had come from books—old pages, stitched together at one end and made of something much rarer than paper. It was parchment, the Story realized—the skin of animals. The pages were large, and the writing on them bore a strong resemblance to that in the oldest of the books downstairs. But this writing wasn't in print. The Story of Everything held one of the pages up to the window and saw that the writing had been done by hand. It was manuscript.

Now he knelt on the floor and emptied out more of the trunk, laying its contents on the floor in the order in which he found them. After the parchment came strips of a different material, held together by a cord. Bamboo, he thought, where had it come from? The writing on the bamboo wasn't in letters at all. It seemed to be in tiny pictures. Further down in the trunk were scrolls made of something else again. The Story knew, without knowing how he knew, that it was papyrus, pressed from the stem of plants. Unrolling one of the scrolls, the Story saw yet another language but recognized that it, too, had been written by hand. Everything in the trunk had.

At the very bottom of the trunk the Story found the oldest and most unusual objects of all—fragments of clay, with markings etched into them. Tablets, he thought, or perhaps pieces of pottery.

Looking at the contents of the trunk, laid out so carefully on the floor, the Story realized he was much older than he had believed. I'm living a printed life, he murmured, but I have also had a life when I was simply written out. A much longer life. The books in the library downstairs covered five hundred years. What he was looking at on the attic floor covered five thousand.

And now the memories came, memories of a life far different from the one he knew. In a place that was hot and arid, the Story found himself looking up at an edge of glaring sunlight. Blocking the sun was the dark and bearded face of a man with a reed in his hand. The reed came closer, the Story felt a scratch, he winced . . . and suddenly he was looking down at a tablet of clay drying in the sun. Etched in the clay were symbols, tiny ones like the markings on the fragments from the trunk. Writing, he realized, the very beginning of it. The very beginning of *him*.

Memories came, too, of the centuries that followed, centuries spent on papyrus, rolled up in scrolls and kept in storage jars. The claustrophobic years, mused the Story; it was the first time he had given them that name. He recalled the stagnant air of the jars, and the deep, fresh breaths he took when he was lifted out of them. He smelled the distant sea again, the salty sea, and saw the library nearby, the huge library with hundreds of thousands of scrolls like him, all of papyrus. The Story remembered, or at least he thought he did, when he was first cut into pages and stitched together on one side. He remembered the monasteries where he'd been copied. He had gotten into the habit of sneaking into them at night to check on the progress that had been made during the day. He'd light a candle and actually touch the script to see if it was dry. Later, he'd gotten bolder and visited the monasteries by day, standing invisible over the shoulders of monks who were dipping their pens into pots of black ink and lifting them over to pages of parchment. He'd been fascinated by the way the width of their strokes could go from that of a ribbon to that of a hair.

But it wasn't the writing that kept the Story coming back. It was the pictures that were painted beside it. It was the reds and the golds and the blues and the greens. It was the intricacy of the designs. It was the story they told.

The pictures had mesmerized the Story of Everything.

And there they were again, there on the floor. The tree and the beast. The snow-covered mountain. The valley filled with mist. The pool of water. The pitch-black sky with stars and moon. The ray of light. The Story held the pictures up to the light the way you would hold old photographs—slowly and meditatively. He saw the king and queen again. The child. The naked man and woman. The touching of the hands. One by one, the Story let the pictures sink in. It dawned on him once more: these things are *me*. And so they were: the smoke, the bloody swords, the eagle and the dove, the healer and the sorcerer, the ring, the ladder to the nether world, the path. All those pictures were part of him.

The light in the attic began to fade, and the Story knew he was running out of time. Methodically, he began to return to the trunk what he had laid on the floor. Only now did he wonder how he could have forgotten all this. The attic, the trunk, the thousands of years in writing.

Once he was downstairs again, the Story of Everything returned to his library and unlocked the glass case. He removed the book he had kept there and laid it on a shelf. In its place he left a fragment of clay, a papyrus scroll, and a page of parchment. On the parchment was a picture, in green and gray and silvery white, of the misty valley and the ray of light. The clay was in the place of honor. Because it represents my birth, he said. That's how, and when, I was born.

The Story of Everything wouldn't forget again. He was getting to know himself.

FIFTEEN

THE trouble with getting to know yourself, of course, is that all of a sudden you want to *be* yourself. After the Story's discovery in the attic, he wanted to be a written thing—or at least to act like one. He wanted to loosen up, to flow like ink. Be an S, he'd tell himself, walk like an S. Or a C. Not so straight. Not so stiff. Not so orthodox. Don't worry about snaky.

It wasn't easy. There were days when the Story tried too hard, tried to do too much too soon. One morning he actually removed his binding and covers. He was okay for a while, but then he felt exposed. He panicked: am *I* coming unglued? And then he wished he'd never opened the trunk in the attic.

But the Story had his good days too, and on those he felt fresh and alive. He felt curious. He felt like opening things. Drawers, cupboards, windows, closets, boxes he hadn't touched in centuries. He felt like opening . . . himself.

On one of his good days, on one of his very best in fact, the Story made a connection. If I've had a previous life, he reasoned, I'll have a life to come. A life in yet another form.

It may have been a coincidence, but not long after the Story of Everything made that connection, a little package arrived in the mail. On its surface were the words, NOW ON CD!!! THE STORY OF EVERYTHING!!! Inside was a small silver disc with a hole in the center.

Within a week of that disc's arrival, the Story of Everything had bought a PC and set it up in his library, next to the glass case that held the record of his birth.

And now, his heart pounding, the Story was sliding the silvery disc into his computer. He watched, he clicked, he waited, and in a few seconds there it was! There *he* was! In crisp and brilliant color, right there on the screen! The Story scrolled around a bit (that was a term he liked), and then he took the fragment of clay from the glass case and found where the words on it were located on the CD. The two sources matched. Not perfectly, but they matched, even though they had been fashioned some five thousand years apart.

Soon more CDs arrived. One that said DELUXE!!! had pictures of the very illustrations the Story had found in his trunk. Another showed the monasteries he had visited and the papyrus library where he had once been stored. Yet another showed him being acted out, with voices that spoke and music that played and pictures that moved, in locations all around the world.

In no time at all, the Story discovered the internet. His followers had been busy there. They had set up sites in his honor, all kinds of them. *Thestoryofeverything.com, thestoryofeverything.net, thetruestoryrevealed.edu*, and so on. Here they chatted, posted, and blogged. They argued, attacked, and defended. They sent e-mail, some of it to him. Each evening the Story would count up the hits, visit the chat rooms, and read the e-mail. But he never joined a conversation or responded to a message. He simply sat in front of his monitor and marveled at it all.

Now, instead of trying to be a written thing, the Story began to imagine himself without a body altogether—as something paperless, and even wireless. What would I look like? he wondered. What would I *be*? A soul, something like that? A pure idea? One day he had this insight: Cyberspace is heaven! I'm going there! I'm never going to die! And then he thought, How lucky can a story get?

His library said it all now. Printed books were there: they spoke of his life in the present. Written fragments were there as well: they spoke of his life in the past. And now there was a computer, a sign of things to come. The screen of that computer glowed throughout the night, like a vigil light. The Story never turned it off.

The Story had found a way, all right. A way to be what he always was, and a way to be it forever. It was the wrong way, but at least it was a way.

SIXTEEN

*O*NLY a Story of Everything? Elise's comment had taken Adam by surprise, and yet he had to concede that, with all the things that needed doing in their lives, and all that needed doing in the world, she had a point.

"You're right," he said, as if to convince himself. But even as he mouthed the words, he felt something going out of him.

Elise didn't see that something go, at least not right away. She and Adam continued to live as they had since Jamie's birth, but now they saw even less of each other. Adam grew more quiet. When Elise pressed, he could not explain himself. They had once talked of getting married, but now the subject rarely came up.

Slowly Elise began to see a different side to the qualities she had loved in Adam. She had loved the way his mind leapt to things, but she couldn't fathom the things it leapt *to*. Why those things, and not others more practical? She had loved his innocence, but not the way it left him blind. Blind not only to the world's politics, but to the politics involved in his own work. If he had her instincts, his career would be going somewhere. Right now, it was stuck in the mud.

"You can't be so naive," she'd say.

Adam wouldn't understand.

Elise's life was stuck too—in the air, like a plane circling an airport, waiting to land. She had had enough of living on the run, not knowing what the next week might bring. A number of friends, turning thirty like her, were opting out of the life they had led for years. A younger generation of activists was moving in. Elise was tired of apartment living. She dreamt of a home and a neighborhood for Jamie, and she wanted them by the time he was ready for school. When she received an offer to work for a legislator in another part of the country, she told Adam that she was going to take the job, and that she was going to take Jamie with her.

"Will you be coming too?" she asked.

Something in the way Elise asked the question told Adam that the answer she hoped for was no. But he didn't really know. There was something else he didn't know: what existed between Elise and the man she was going to work for. Because he didn't know these things, Adam took stock of what he did know. He did know that Elise was right about his work, though not about the reason for its going nowhere. He did know that his mind would always leap to things that others found impractical. He knew that awe would often leave him blind. He knew that he was a dreamer and Elise a doer. Mostly, he knew that Jamie was more like his mother than like his father.

"No," Adam replied several days later.

Elise's sigh of relief was almost audible. She assured Adam that he would always be Jamie's father, and then she worked with him on detailed and generous plans for taking care of their son. There was no contention. Nor, at the airport, when the time finally came to say good-bye, was there any wrenching in the separation, at least none that showed.

Driving home that day, Adam felt a weight lifting from his shoulders. His thoughts turned to the rest of his life. He was, incredibly, thirty-three years old. He had hoped there would be a double helix in his future, another dazzling structure in the world of nature that he would be the first to see. He had hoped to develop a "theory," or establish a "paradigm," or at least come up with a new "hypothesis." But after ten years he had done none of those things. His colleagues considered him a keen and exacting empiricist. They said that he was promising. But, in Adam's mind, he was nothing more than a collector of minutiae.

In the year that followed, when he'd be flying home from seeing Jamie, Adam gradually saw why he had developed no theories, no paradigms, nor even one hypothesis. The questions in his mind were all too big. Instead of trying to crack the genetic code, he was wondering more and more of late, *Why is there such a code?* And were there other codes on other planets? And were there other evolutions?

Maybe, he said one day, I should look into a different story, a bigger story, a story as big as the universe itself. Maybe, he said, I should look into the Story of Matter.

He wrote some letters and, in short order, received some replies. One was from a group of astronomers who found his background "intriguing." They wondered if he had an interest in the birth of stars. Some conversations followed; some analogies were developed. Adam recalled the star involved in Galileo's story, the one that flared up so intensely in 1604. At the time observers called it a "nova" because they thought it was a new star, the flare-up being its birth. Later, astronomers realized that the flare-up was its death, and they renamed it a "supernova."

That star got Adam thinking. It drove home the fact that all the stars in the sky, all the stars he knew so well—the ones in the Big and Little Dippers, the ones in Gemini, the ones in Orion, the ones in all the constellations he had learned as a boy—would one day die. They were not eternal. Even Polaris, the one he always looked for first, even Polaris had had a birth and would eventually have a death. It struck Adam that stars *evolved*, just as life on earth did. They had their births, their deaths, their course of life in between. They had their generations.

Adam's interest grew, but he wasn't convinced that he should make a change until he saw some especially beautiful photographs of nebulae. Nebulae were brilliant clouds of gas and dust lurking in the dark of outer space. They were the graveyards of stars that had died and the nurseries of stars being born. And they were something to behold, with a strange and distant beauty that called to Adam from afar. Adam could not give himself to something unless it called like that—unless it called like the Owl Nebula, a ghostlike face that stared at him from deep in space, never blinking, never turning away. Or the Horsehead, rising jet-black against a background of red, looking exactly like a knight on a chessboard. Or the Butterfly, with delicate, transparent wings. Or the Crab, or the Eagle, or the Tarantula. Inkblots of red and green and blue and white splattered in the depths of space. Inkblots where stars had died, where stars were being born.

As soon as he saw those photographs, Adam's "maybe" became "of course." Of course he should make a change. Of course he should take up the Story of Matter. On a day when Jamie sounded especially happy on the phone, Adam made a decision: he would go to school again and study astronomy.

SEVENTEEN

AS Adam was leaving for his second schooling, space probes were leaving the earth for destinations farther and farther away. And as he followed his charted course, they did too, flying past Venus and Mercury, past Mars and Jupiter and Saturn. All the while, they sent back pictures of thick and murky clouds, ancient river valleys, giant canyons, and mountains that dwarfed the ones on earth. Now Adam saw, up close, the moons of Jupiter, the very four that were specks to Galileo. Reddish Io, smooth and icy Europa, brightly cratered Callisto, and Ganymede, larger even than the earth's moon. He saw rings around Saturn so thin they looked from the side like razors. He reminded himself that everything he saw had had a birth, and would one day have a death.

School was different the second time around. Adam was older than his fellow students, older even than some of his teachers. He was wiser too. He saw what he hadn't seen before—what Elise had called the "politics" of science. He saw how fierce the competition was, how bitter the disappointments. He saw what it took to do the business of science, and though he didn't relish the business, he did it. He learned the ropes, at least a few of them.

But the ropes were nothing like the stars, which were what he had come to see in the first place. And the stars did not disappoint Adam. He did indeed see them in their birth, as dense clumps of glowing gas and dust collapsed inward and ignited in nuclear fusion—in stardom. He saw stars, once born, approach their youth, white hot, flamboyant, hanging out in clusters. He saw old stars too, ancient ones ballooning in size, turning red, shedding their outer shells, awaiting a violent and eerily beautiful death. Adam saw stars, not just in birth and death, but in all the seasons of their life.

It was a long way from the stories of princesses riding on the backs of Bulls and Winged Horses springing up from blood, a long way from Taurus and Pegasus and being a child. It was now the Story of Matter, told in the language of science. Adam learned that Story, not with the telescope of his boyhood, but with amazing new instruments that captured all kinds of radiation, gamma rays and x-rays, light waves and radio waves. As a boy, all he had seen was the narrow band of radiation called light. Now Adam learned that light held but a fraction of the story, that the universe was full of "dark" matter, and "dark" energy, and holes as powerful as they were "black."

His colleagues called the Story of Matter the "new" cosmology. More than anything else, that cosmology said the *universe* had evolved, the whole of it, just as life on earth had, just as stars and planets had. In the beginning, the universe was just a point— smaller than the head of a pin, smaller than an atom on the head of that pin, smaller than the smallest thing you can think of. But it was also incredibly dense. It flared out. Bang! It "inflated."

Space and time shot out faster than light could ever hope to travel. Within moments, simple atoms began to form, hydrogen and helium. Galaxies took shape—and stars. The stars created carbon in their furnaces, and then they blew apart and formed again: a second generation. A third generation came, and now the universe had iron and all the heavy elements. It had what was needed for planets. It had what was needed for Life. It had what was needed . . . for Adam. Was it planned that way? Was it "designed"? Adam couldn't say. What he realized was this: His roots were out in space. *He* was made of stardust.

Long before Adam's second schooling was complete, it wasn't schooling anymore. Adam had become a colleague of his teachers, a full-fledged member of their team, though far from its key player. As the years passed, things kept getting better, for the team at least. They had spotted galaxies running into other galaxies, and they had seen the myriads of infant stars that those collisions spawned. Now, in the excitement of their discovery, they were engrossed in explanation.

Some of the excitement, however, was lost on Adam. By the middle of his forties, his mind was wandering off again. Wandering *in*, to tell the truth, to a place where he saw that *his* space and *his* time were slipping away. Every now and then he would smile at his youthful dream of finding a pattern in nature that no one else had seen before. Every now and then he'd think about the breath of God. And then he would wonder, What am I doing panning the dust of galaxies, searching for infant stars?

EIGHTEEN

J AMIE grew. Each summer he would visit his father, and each summer Adam would take him to an old observatory that wasn't used much anymore. There he would show his son what he himself had seen as a child, but now through eyes more powerful. Things like the polar caps on Mars and a dust storm there, the red spot on Jupiter, gaps in the rings of Saturn, the greenish disks that were Uranus and Neptune. On one occasion, he even showed him a comet, its glittering tail swaying in the solar wind.

But most of their time was spent on the moon. Adam led Jamie over its surface as if it were spread out on a table before them. He taught him the familiar names: the craters Tycho and Clavius, Mare Serenitatis, Montes Apenninus, Vallis Rheita. The two of them practically climbed the mountains at the edge of lunar night. "This is where a meteor struck. Down there is where a human landed," Adam would say. Whenever they spotted a crater, or a new volcano, or some softly mounded lava flow, he would say, "I wonder where it came from. I wonder how it got there." Because Adam knew very well where those things came from, it suddenly dawned on him: His grandfather must have known too. He must have known how a cloud was formed, or how a seashell landed in a rock, or a freckle on a face. Then Adam realized, for the first time in his life, why his grandfather had asked all those questions.

Adam could have spent entire nights showing Jamie around the moon, but Jamie's eyes would eventually grow heavy, and Adam would have to carry his slumping body back to the car.

"Can I bring a friend?" Jamie asked one year when the time came to visit his father. He was almost in his teens now, and it was his way of saying, "Enough of the moon."

"Of course," said Adam.

That summer Jamie brought two friends, and Adam took them camping. Now he was asking different questions. What if it rains? What if someone gets sick? What did I forget? He must have answered the questions well, because the boys had a great, though soggy, adventure. The following summer it was three friends. Each year, as the boys grew, the adventures became more rugged. Jamie and his friends wanted greater challenges: canoeing; long, backbreaking portages; surviving with a minimum of gear. Adam struggled to keep up with them. But he liked the way they took charge, and the way they formed a bond, and the way they made sure to include the "old man," even if, on occasion, it meant taking the easy way out.

In the summer before he went off to college, Jamie told his father that he'd like to spend a day with him. No friends this time, just the two of them. They could hike a trail that had been one of Adam's favorites.

It drizzled on and off that day—a soft, windless rain that was more like a heavy fog. At the trailhead, where water had soaked into beds of fallen needles, there was a rich smell of pine, which faded as the trail climbed upward into rockier terrain. Soon Jamie and Adam were following a river upstream, looking down steep banks as it gushed through a gorge below. Even with the gray sky, the water was a luminescent blue.

Jamie did most of the talking. He talked about his mother, and what his life with her life was like, and how he wished she'd taken the time to have another child. He talked about his "other" father. It took him a while to say so, but eventually he did: He admired the man. He admired Adam, too, but he really didn't understand the work he did. Jamie's word was "after." He didn't understand what Adam was "after."

They were at a place where the river spilled into a deep pool that was green with moss and trees. The path narrowed after that, so Adam went ahead. It gave him time to think. He wasn't sure himself what he was "after," so how could he explain it to his son? Passing through a grove of spruce, he came to see that Jamie wasn't looking for an explanation. He was "after" something else. The trail then opened to a vista that exposed them to the mist. Before them lay a lake that was the river's source. A mink or muskrat—they couldn't tell which—was feeding on the shore.

Jamie broke the silence. "I'd like to do what he does," he finally said, referring to his other father. "With my life, I mean." He was very clear about this, very certain. It was what he had come to say.

Adam thought back to the day when he had sat by a river and talked with a teacher, watching autumn leaves float slowly away. Still looking at the gray and misty lake, he said to Jamie, "You have a gift. You have to honor it."

The sky lightened a bit, they lingered for a while, and then they turned back. Jamie took the lead now: back through the grove of spruce, back beside the pool of green, back along the ridge that overlooked the gorge. Adam felt an uncoupling, the freeing of a nature that was different from his own. By the time they reached the trailhead, Adam had caught up with the meaning of the day. He understood what Jamie had been after, and he was glad for it. He was glad that his blessing had mattered.

NINETEEN

I N the months that followed the walk in the mist, Adam drifted back to the observatory where he had taken Jamie when he was growing up. His mind could wander there, especially on cold wintry evenings when the sky grew dark early and he had a mug of coffee steaming by his side.

He was alone in his life, now at age fifty. Alone in the universe, it seemed, a link without a chain. He had loved no woman since Elise, for none had known him the way that she had. He and Elise did not belong together, Adam knew that. But their separation had left him in a quandary: if he did not belong with her, with whom did he possibly belong?

Adam wasn't given to finding fault in people, in others, or himself, but that began to change now. Now he began to see a flaw in himself, in his very character. And more than a flaw, a "fault line," he told himself in darker moments. Something in Adam could move very abruptly on people he loved, on things he loved, and in no time see them as alien. And so he'd let them go. There had been no fight from him when Elise and Jamie left, no protest, no staking of a claim, no hanging on. Just a farewell. Nor did Adam, even now, disavow that farewell. He did not say, I should have acted differently, I should have tried to make it work. All he said was, Move. Find a different love.

Adam didn't understand this flaw. He made no connection to the sorrow and the anger in himself, to the place that was covered with branches of pine. But he knew the flaw ran deep, and he was seeing that it led to isolation. And perhaps that was what he really wanted. Perhaps seclusion was his other love. Perhaps it was solitude.

Thus it came about that on dark and wintry nights, his hands cupping his coffee for warmth, his eyes staring into its steam, Adam found solitude to spare. He saw his life taking different paths in those wisps of steam. He saw that he'd gone "out there" twice now, once in his youth and once in middle age. Each time, he'd found astonishing things, but not the thing he wanted most, not the pattern hiding in nature, waiting to be uncovered. In astronomy, as in biology, he'd become a keen observer of detail, but not a theorizer. Again, he wondered why. Again, he asked if he'd been led astray by questions that were just too big.

And, for a second time, Adam answered yes. But there was more to it, something greater than scale, something deeper than character, something far below any flaw or fault line.

That something was *story*. Adam had no idea how often the word entered his mind and how seldom it escaped. He didn't know how many beginnings and middles and endings were trapped inside of him, or how they kept lining up, now this way, now that. He didn't realize that, at his core, Matter was a *story*, not a science. Life was a story, too, not "biology." It was narrative, all of it, but Adam didn't know it. He was fifty years old, and he still didn't know how his own mind worked, what its deepest desire was.

In a bookstore one day, Adam came across a Chinese poet who wrote about a place called Cold Mountain. Cold Mountain was a real place, an actual mountain on China's eastern coast. The poet lived there between the eighth and ninth centuries. But Cold Mountain was also a spiritual place, a destination for the heart.

The Cold Mountain poet spoke to Adam:

> I climb the road to Cold Mountain,
> The road to Cold Mountain that never ends.
> The valleys are long and strewn with stones.
> The streams hard and bunched with thick grass.
> Moss is slippery, though no rain has fallen.
> Pines sigh, but it isn't the wind.
> Who can break from the snares of the world
> And sit with me among the white clouds? . . .
>
> I think of all the places I've been,
> Who would guess I'd end up under a pine tree,
> Clasping my knees in the whispering cold?

As an astronomer, Adam had spent a lot of time on mountains, on cold ones too, but he had always been looking "out there." The poet's Cold Mountain was "in there," and now it called to Adam the way that nebulae once did. But Adam wasn't sure how to make the journey.

> Now it is that, straying from the path,
> You ask your shadow, "which way from here?"

Adam asked that very question, but he got no answer, so he had to go it alone. He began to make changes in his life, small ones at first. Whenever he attended a scientific meeting, no matter where in the world it was held, he set aside time to visit a mountain. Not a cold one, nor even an actual one, but some sacred place of revelation. A cave, perhaps, or a river, a tree, or just some higher ground. A place where someone had heard a voice, or received a law, or been enlightened, or simply gained perspective. Adam was trying to gain perspective too.

He visited places of human design as well, sacred places of religion. Temples and shrines, cathedrals and mosques. Adam stood inside these places. He sat in them. He knelt. He bowed. He saw how stone could create an interior, shape it, and send it upward to a single point. And he wondered, Can I shape the space within myself in the very same way? Can I let that space *be* shaped?

He began to read Scriptures, to practice disciplines. Not all at once, and not consistently, but as time allowed and by way of experiment. At odd moments he made notes in a kind of journal.

He collected sayings there. He wrote down prayers and insights. He yielded to a kind of grace. Months turned into years, spare time into sacred time. Adam's journal became the story of a spirit, "a page in earth's Story of Spirit" (he wrote that in the journal early on). It became an accounting, too—of Four Noble Truths, of Five Pillars, of an Eightfold Path, of Ten Commandments. But in the end Adam's journal became a search for One Thing Above All, for the pearl of great price, for the essence.

As the years passed, the entries in his journal became shorter. Even the very words did. More and more, Adam wanted to condense, to distill. He wanted to *be* still. And there were times when he was, times when he was nothing but a space enclosed in stone. Nothing but an eye. An I.

One spring Adam went to the desert, where he stayed, all alone, in a cabin that belonged to a friend. He had just turned sixty, and he wanted to empty his mind of clutter. He wanted to discover "which way from here."

> Ten years now he hasn't gone home;
> he's even forgotten the road he came by.

His friend's cabin sat in a wide valley, near cliffs that looked like they'd been drenched in watercolors. Early each morning, Adam would look at the reds in those cliffs and feel their sandpaper surface. He'd feel the lavenders, the whites, the blacks. Then he'd explore the valley floor. Marigolds were in bloom, and sore-eyed poppies, and little desert stars, and spikes of lupine. Cactuses too. Yellows and reds and creams and blues surrounded by needles and spines. In the afternoon, as the sun scorched the earth, Adam would retreat to the cabin, only to emerge again at night, in the chill, when the sky had lowered itself and he could practically touch its stars. By the time he fell asleep, Adam would have found the emptiness he craved.

One morning at dawn, a low shaft of sunlight streaked through the valley where Adam was staying and outlined every flower, rock, and pebble. It was a solitary ray, and it lasted no more than a minute. But in that minute there awoke in Adam a solitary longing. Why that? he asked. Why now? It made no difference: he might as well have told the sun to go back down. For in that minute Adam learned which way from here. He learned what he had yet to do in life, perhaps what he was born to do. I am to speak a Story, he said, and he knew which story it was.

TWENTY

THE Story of Everything had discovered Google. One day he typed in "writing," and then he typed in "history," and a few clicks later he discovered what you already know: there was a time when writing did not exist. Five thousand years ago, maybe ten, depending on what you mean by writing. The Story made a deduction: I must have had another life, back before the others. There must have been a time when I was just a spoken thing. An oral thing, and nothing else.

Soon the Story wanted to have a memory of his life in speech—not a deduction, but an actual memory. Some hint, if only a word or two, of what his life back then was like. But the Story could recover nothing of his spoken life, and nothing that he opened in his house, nothing from the trunk, nothing from a closet or a cupboard, held any clues. And there was no place else to look.

Except . . . the basement, he realized one evening. The Story got a flashlight, climbed down the creaky stairs, and started to look around. How long had it been? he wondered. He spotted the furnace, about where he remembered it, then ducts overhead, then pipes. Cobwebs were everywhere. Down his light went to the floor, over to a drain, then to a wall, then . . . a door. Now he remembered: wine! It was the wine cellar.

The door squeaked when he opened it, and the Story recognized that squeak. Opposite the door was a wall of racks, and the Story began to check them, one by one. Empty, every one of them. But on the lowest rack, at its very end, he spotted a lone bottle of wine. It had no label, no cork, only a kind of waxy seal. The Story had no idea where it had come from, or how it had gotten to his cellar. Had it been a gift? Had he bought it? Or maybe "borrowed" it on one of his trips to a monastery? The Story had no way of knowing, so he did the only thing he could. He got a knife and a glass and opened one last thing.

Incredibly, the wine was good—so good, in fact, that the Story had a second glass. And a third. The taste, he decided, was "earthy." He found a place to sit, right there in the cellar. He turned off the lights, lifted the wine to his nose, and let that earthy taste do things to his memory.

At first, it brought back smells of other wines, older ones. And then . . . what was it? . . . ink, ink on metal type, a smell that made him shiver. Then came candle wax, warm and fragrant. Smoke came, he could practically taste it. Then sweat, and now the Story felt a rhythm in the ground, and for a moment he actually heard a kind of chant, and he could have sworn that the words of that chant were the very words he kept upstairs, locked in a case of glass. He could have sworn that he had found the memory he craved.

That should have ended the matter, but it did not. For as the chant faded, something lingered in the darkness. It was like a scent, faint but very real. It seemed to come closer. The Story tried to speak, but a finger touched his lips. And then he got a memory he hadn't craved, hadn't even known about. A memory not of sound, but of Silence. A memory of his life before he ever spoke a word.

Silence. She had been a constant then. She had been a lover. She had lain with him and breathed with him and then they'd set off on a journey through the cosmos, his very first. Out to the edges of the earth they'd sped, down to the caverns in the sea, up to the firmament on high, in to the innermost truths. The memories were coming back now, there in the darkness of the cellar: The naked man and woman, and the child. The valley, filled with mist, where they lived. The place where rain was stored. The place where snow was. The pillars of stone that held up the earth. The massive doors, locked with a single bolt, that kept the sea from breaking through (you could actually hear them groan). The crystalline orbs that bore the stars and planets (how it felt to touch them!). The path to the home of Light. The sound of the orders it gave each day to dawn. The hole where Darkness lived. The beast down there, the smoke, the bloody swords, the grisly goings-on.

A Story and a Silence, that's what they'd been. Seeing it all. Opposites and complements. He had searched for solid truths, absolutes, ultimate foundations. She had sought the edge of every mystery, never stopping till she got there. Not to the edge before the edge, but to the very edge, the one before the things you couldn't know. And then she had bowed before the Great Unknown.

Amazing, thought the Story, we never said a word. But when their journey was complete, Silence left. And then the Story spoke. In fact, he couldn't stop the flow of words.

Glass shattered on the floor. The Story startled awake, as though from a dream. When he turned on a light, he saw pieces of glass by the side of his chair. He saw wine that had spilled. But he saw, and he sensed, nothing else.

How much had he drunk? he wondered.

The next morning, the Story went to his library and sat again in his favorite chair. He didn't know what had happened the night before, or why it had happened, or even *if* it had happened. But something had changed, something deep within.

He looked around. He saw books squeezed together on shelves, shoulder-to-shoulder, barely able to breathe. He saw pieces of clay lying under glass, looking like mummies. He saw a computer's never-ending glow. Dead, thought the Story. The place was a museum, a prison. And he'd been living there.

Living? There now passed through the Story's mind all the forms in which he had existed. His life in speech, his life in writing, his life in print, his life in cyberspace. None could compare with the time he had spent in silence. No one followed him around back then, with pen and parchment. No one rolled him up at night and stuffed him in a jar. No one bound him in a book. No one scolded, "You have to be consistent! You have to get the story straight! You have to write it . . . right!"

Though the Story of Everything never understood what happened in the basement of his soul, he claimed it. He claimed all of it, whatever it was: the silence in himself, the touching, the movement, the awe, the mystery, the bow. The complement, the other half. And as he staked his claim, the chair in which he sat became uncomfortable. It was painful to remain.

And so the Story rose from that chair. He unplugged the computer and turned toward the door. He knew his place wasn't here anymore, not in this room. It wasn't in a book, or on a piece of parchment, or up in cyberspace. It wasn't spoken, written, printed, digitized. It was—the word simply came—*enfleshed*.

TWENTY-ONE

WITH a sense of being whole again—in his memory, deep within his being—the Story of Everything entered a state of quiet expectation, as if he were waiting to hear from someone. And in that state he began to sense an unusual longing. It wasn't a longing *in* him, but rather a longing *for* him. It came from the outside, and he was its object. But he had no idea where it was coming from.

Each day the longing returned. Finally, the Story said, "I've got to find it. I've got to know where it's coming from." But he had no idea how to look for a longing. Or where.

He tried nevertheless, in the places he knew best—the attic, the basement of course, and last of all, the library. He emptied the trunk once again, laying out its contents in perfect order on the floor. The longing wasn't there. He went down to the cellar and turned off his flashlight, sipping what remained of the wine. Nothing. He took books off library shelves, dozens of them that he picked at random, and flipped through their pages. He found no longing. Finally, he tried the internet. He clicked, he chatted, he revved the search engines, he followed the links. But the longing wasn't up in cyberspace.

Then the Story recalled that there had been longing in Venice, back in Galileo's day. He recalled how powerful it had been, and how encompassing. And it all seemed to come from a single telescope.

The next morning, the Story rose early, ate quickly, took a deep breath, and—before he could change his mind—headed off to Venice. He was going to find that telescope. When he closed the door to his house, he had the strange feeling that he would never see the place again.

Once in Venice, the Story paddled for days and made inquiries of anyone who would talk to him. But he didn't find the telescope, not there at any rate. He found it further south, in Florence, on display in a museum, standing at an angle above a long Latin inscription. It looked so very small.

The museum was full of scientific instruments, and soon the Story of Everything was absorbed in them. Balances and barometers, compasses and clocks, pendulums and prisms, sectors and sextants, vacuum tubes and tubes of mercury. The signs said not to touch them, but the Story did anyway. He touched telescopes more powerful than Galileo's. Some used lenses, some used mirrors, some used both. Anything to concentrate light. One had a long taut wire running from its lens to its eyepiece. Several had eyepieces on the side, not the back. They reminded the Story of the one he had first looked into.

So taken was the Story by what he was finding that he forgot what he was looking for. He became obsessed with telescopes, and he got very good at finding them, all kinds of them, all over the world. He found them under smooth white domes, high on mountaintops, up above the clouds. He found them in clusters of twos and threes and fours. He found them in airplanes and balloons. He found them heading out to space, sending pictures back to earth. He found them circling the earth, like little moons. One in particular was able to see billions of miles, billions of light years, they said. Things had come a long way since Galileo.

Looking down on a desert one day, the Story noticed a Y-shaped pattern of dishes pointing upward, forming lines that stretched for miles. Radio telescopes, he learned to his amazement. They were "seeing" what you couldn't see with eyes, or perhaps "hearing" it: radiation that lay outside of light, of wavelengths longer than light. Incredible, thought the Story. He hadn't known those wavelengths existed. And just as he was saying it, he discovered telescopes for wavelengths shorter than light, for x-rays, gamma rays, and the like. How much there was to see, he marveled, how little our eyes took in!

The Story found longing, too, longing to spare. Scientists fought just to use those telescopes. They argued over what they saw with them. They wanted desperately to *know*. For a while, the Story was caught up in all of it—until he realized that what he had found was a longing for this, and a longing for that, but not a longing for Everything.

Why not? the Story wondered. Why not a longing for Everything? And even as he asked the question, he thought he knew the answer: Everything was just too big. There was just too much of it.

When he had first seen Everything in silence, there had been an earth, a sun, a moon, some stars, some planets. That was it. It wasn't even called a "universe" then. You started at the center and went out to the edges, to the boundaries beyond which nothing existed. But everything was different now. The earth was the center of nothing that mattered, the sun that it circled was the center of little else, and though the galaxy that harbored the sun contained a hundred billion other suns, it wasn't itself a center. Just one of a billion or trillion galaxies. And the universe that held all these billions and trillions was itself expanding. And the expansion itself was picking up steam, or so at least it seemed. How could a Story of Everything get to the edges now? The edges were faster than he was. Maybe there were no edges. Maybe everything was infinite.

And maybe Newton was right, the Story added. He had seen Sir Isaac's words in a museum: "To explain all of nature is too difficult a task for any one man or even any one age."

There's got to be another way, the Story thought. And he found one: to think small, not big. To see the world in a grain of sand. To find the tiniest thing there is and then learn everything there is to learn about it.

So the Story got a microscope, an old one that he lifted from a museum. (He had every intention, of course, of bringing it back.)

The microscope had but a single lens. The Story was intrigued by what it revealed, but he wasn't overwhelmed. So he got a bigger microscope, a better one with compound lenses. He saw more, but still he wasn't overwhelmed. So he went on. Eventually he found microscopes that used electron beams and magnetic fields instead of light and lenses of glass. And then he saw an atom.

The atom was small, but it wasn't the smallest thing there was.

In a huge circular tunnel buried in the ground, a tunnel that extended for miles, the Story discovered particles smaller than atoms racing around at breakneck speeds and crashing into each other. Out of the crashes there sometimes streaked even smaller particles, if only for a moment. "Gluons, leptons, mesons, muons," said the scientists who were engineering the demolition derby. "Quarks." They were the smallest things of all.

But what were these things? Forces? Building blocks? Geometric points? Chunks of space-time? Strings? Membranes? Scientists would gather for the better part of a week, debate and compare notes, then throw up their hands.

The Story would throw up his hands too, for these scientists were working in nanometers and attometers. A nanometer was a billionth of a meter. A attometer was a billionth of a billionth. It was .000000000000000001 of a meter, .000000000000001 of a dot. If the scientists couldn't understand .000000000000001 of a dot, the Story lamented, how was he supposed to understand everything there was?

I'm getting nowhere, he said one afternoon, sitting dejectedly on the ground above a section of tunnel. Particles were zooming around beneath him, and scientists were trying to steer them into each other. Earlier in the day, he had overheard hallway talk about "everything." He had heard the very word, and he had stopped to listen more closely. Bring the two together, the scientists were saying, the theory of the biggest things and the theory of the smallest. "General relativity" and "quantum mechanics": make them one and call what you create the theory of everything. It all made sense because the vast, vast universe was once the tiniest thing there was.

Standing in the shadows, listening in on that conversation, the Story of Everything had actually felt his heart begin to pound. And for a while he believed that he had found what he was looking for. But then he realized that "everything" wasn't Everything at all. No one in the halls said a word about Life. No one said a word about Spirit.

Soon the Story was thinking about what he hadn't heard, and about Life in particular. He remembered the bones that the *Evolution* books had dumped on his floor, and he set out to find more of them. And find more he did, older ones than in Darwin's day, and stranger ones. On the island of Madagascar, he found fragments of dinosaurs with parrot beaks—rhynchosaurs, they called them. In the quarries of China, under flaked away stone, there were skeletons—whole ones—of dinosaurs with feathers. They looked like turkeys, but they weren't birds. In the foothills of the Himalayas, he saw the remains of whales that walked, and even ran, on land. They were fifty million years old.

Nor was it simply bones that the Story found. It was bugs—termites and bees and weevils perfectly preserved in amber from twenty-five, forty, even a hundred million years ago. It was a flower from fifty million years ago, frozen brown in rock, the veins in its petals still visible. In Africa, it was a trail of footprints set in hardened mud that was three, maybe four million years old. One set of prints was left by an adult, another by a child. Both were humanlike. A fossil of care, thought the Story: an adult had been walking beside a child, perhaps holding its hand. In China, he saw a block of sandstone that was seventy-five million years old. Inside was a dinosaur's nest that contained the bones of the dinosaur as well as the eggs on which the dinosaur was sitting. What a tale they told! thought the Story. He pictured a mother or father refusing to leave the nest in the midst of a giant sandstorm. Another fossil of care.

In his travels, the Story of Everything came upon story after story like that, amazing tales about the development of Life. In Greenland, and again in Australia, he saw in rocks the relics of one-celled creatures that were nearly four *billion* years old, almost as old as the earth itself. He saw in a piece of debris from Mars what looked like a tiny organism, long since expired. He saw massive, gouged-out craters where asteroids had struck and snuffed out species after species, making room for newcomers.

The numbers staggered the Story's mind. Fifty million. A hundred million. Four *billion*. Life was older than he had ever thought possible. Why hadn't he seen these fossils before, when he had first explored the cosmos? Why hadn't he seen the creatures they were fossils *of*?

Nor was it just fossils that left the Story reeling. It was living creatures, odd ones, doing things he never thought Life could—or even should. Snails were mating in the shallows of a lake, but cloning out in the deep! Fish were changing sex! Bacteria were slurping poison in the scalding waters of thermal springs—and loving it! But they were also colonizing vents of gas in the cold, black canyons of the sea. Worms were down there, too, wriggling in the muck. And jellies, pulsing, luminescing, trailing tentacles like strands of gossamer—under tons of pressure! He had been in the deep before. How had he missed these creatures? How had he missed the fish with horns, the plants with mouths? And what about the mouse he saw back on land? It had a human ear, or something like a human ear, growing out of its back. The Story found it in a laboratory, next to a rabbit that glowed in the dark.

Life, the Story decided, was not what it seemed his first time around.

In America, he came across the beginnings of an explanation. Rows and rows of computers were working day and night to make a map of the human genome. They were laying out the *a*'s, the *c*'s, the *g*'s, and the *t*'s in precisely the right order, over ten thousand letters per minute. They were working out the codes of other creatures, too, of bacteria and viruses, of worms and flies and flowers and mice. They were showing how little of our DNA was actually composed of genes, how little it took to make a human being (not much more than what it took to make a worm or mouse), how much of that was common to all of Life. The day would come, the Story saw, when the fossil record in the earth and the living record in the DNA would stand side by side and tell the whole Story of Life.

But even then something would be missing, thought the Story. Matter would be missing. Spirit would.

In the laboratories of Life, the Story realized that he had found longing as great as any he had encountered. Scientists there wanted to *know*, and they wanted even more—to have a say in what Life was doing, to affect the course it was taking. But none of the longings the Story found was the one he was looking for. None was a longing for Everything.

Maybe I should try a place of Spirit, the Story said one afternoon, as a roomful of computers droned on. He slipped out of the room and set off on yet another pilgrimage. It proved to be shorter than the others, for he was already familiar with much of what he saw—not only with the places, but with what had happened in them. Standing on a mountain, or in a cave, or by the sea, or in a desert, or under a particular tree, the Story recalled the times when God had spoken or insights had been granted. He recalled a temptation being overcome, an attachment being broken, a self being emptied, a Self being met. Remembering these events was easy, for the memories were some of the oldest ones he had.

But there were new sights too, places of "art" and "learning" and "justice" and "religion" that didn't exist before, with arches and pillars and spires and domes, with stone that looked like lace, with storytelling glass and tile, with silvers and golds and greens and whites. The Story had heard about these places and even been inside a few of them. But he had no idea how they had multiplied. Or how stunning they could be, or how much reverence they could command.

The Story entered these places, just as he had the laboratories of Matter and Life. Those of religion intrigued him. At times he found quiet inside, the stillness of the Absolute. At times he found deafening sound—music and shouting and song. There were speakers of all kinds. Some invoked authority, others authenticity. Some were ready to condemn, others ready to embrace. Some were drawn to certainty, others drawn to mystery. There were worshipers and lovers in these places, seekers and believers, those who were trying to find the Spirit and those convinced they had. In one of them, the Story saw a man writing in a journal, but paid him no attention.

The Story listened closely to what was going on, but he never heard a word about gamma rays or quarks. No one said "Matter," except when Matter was the enemy. And though they talked of Life, it was a different kind of Life, with different measuring sticks. No one breathed a single a, or c, or g, or t.

The Story found longing in these places, and it was deep and strong. But it was not a longing for Everything.

He ended up one night on a cliff overlooking the ocean. He could trudge no farther. Small lights were rising in the distance, then disappearing into the dark. There must have been an airport farther down the coastline. The Story thought of going home, but where was home now, and what was home? Not the place he had left a year ago.

Was it only a year? The Story went over all the things he had found. Not just trillions of other suns, not just fossils of care, not just stone that looked like lace. He had also found qubits and magnetars, proteomes and morganucodontids, ids and memes, e-commerce and virtual reality, fundamentalism and postmodernism. And thousands of other things he couldn't even name. He had, in truth, found too much. He had come across a glut of information. The problem was . . . he wasn't gluttonous. Knowledge had exploded, people kept on saying. The problem was . . . he'd rather stay in one piece.

I'm not a know-it-all, the Story realized that night on the cliff. I'm just a Story of Everything. In the background, airplanes kept rising into the darkness. Zombies, thought the Story, coming and going, one after the other. Always on the move, never allowed to sit still.

For him it had been a year of movement, and on this particular night, the Story felt there was a lot to be said for sitting still. There was a lot to be said for solid ground. For ultimate foundations. For cliffs of granite, like the one on which he was perched.

But where was solid ground these days? Where were ultimate foundations? The very cliff on which he sat was floating on a plate, for goodness sake. Whole continents were drifting. Nothing was anchored anymore. Nothing stood still all the way down.

For the first time in his life, the Story of Everything wondered if there was a place anymore for someone like himself. Sitting there beside the ocean, watching airplanes come and go, he suddenly felt as though he belonged to a different era. He felt very old. What now? he wondered. Which way from here? He rose from his floating cliff and did the only thing he knew how to do anymore: just move. Just get up and move. Like a zombie, if he had to. This time he moved, on aching feet, to the airport.

TWENTY-TWO

WHEREVER it lays me down, the Story was saying when he arrived, wherever it lays me down. "It" was the wind, and the Story of Everything had decided to throw his fate to it. He would search for the source no longer. He would surrender to the wind and let it carry him to his destiny.

It was past midnight when the Story of Everything began checking monitors for departures. It didn't matter where a flight was going, just *so* it was going, the sooner the better. But with the wind, not into it.

With the wind meant east, across the ocean, and the Story quickly found an eastbound flight. C-13, he said to no one in particular, and slipped through security the way any story would. The few travelers at C-13 were staring blankly ahead, occasionally checking their watches. A television set flickered in the background. Crumpled newspapers lay unread on rows of black chairs. On one of those chairs sat a man who was writing on a pad of paper. A small bag lay at his feet. Something about the man seemed oddly familiar to the Story of Everything, but he couldn't put his finger on what it was.

The boarding call was announced, the Story went to the end
of the passenger line, and he walked, unseen, past the attendant
who was taking tickets. Inside the plane were plenty of empty
seats. The Story found one on the aisle and sank into it. He
noticed that the man with the notepad was next to the window.
His bag lay on the seat between them. The Story saw a name on
the tag, but it didn't ring a bell.

Eventually the man stowed his bag and laid his pad at his side.
The Story looked over and saw that it was full of calculations.
Near the top of the page, boxed off in a corner, were the letters
L, M, and S. They had been written several times, in different con-
figurations. S, M, L . . . M, L, S . . . S, L, M . . . variations like
that. No matter how the letters were arranged, however, they
always pointed to the letter E.

The plane backed out of the terminal and taxied to the runway. The man stared outside his window, then returned to his calculations. On a fresh page he wrote an M, then an L, then an S,
only this time he followed them with dates. It looked like this:

> M . . . . January 1
> L . . . . September 15
> S . . . . December 31

Curious, thought the Story. Now the plane was speeding
down the runway, and the Story was craning over the man's shoul-

der. Calculations snaked all over the page. The man studied them for a while, then frowned. After December 31 he wrote:

11:58 P.M.

Two minutes to midnight, thought the Story of Everything. The man wasn't done. A moment later he wrote:

S of E . . . . . December 31, 11:59 P.M.

S of E? Impossible. The Story looked again at the face of the man. It was as intent as ever. He looked again at the time on the page: one minute to midnight on the last day of the year.

TWENTY-THREE

OVER the next few hours the man drifted in and out of sleep. But the Story, exhausted though he was, could not get his eyes to stay shut. His mind kept seeing that S of E. The sense of familiarity kept getting stronger. All through the dark hours of early morning, the Story of Everything tried to forget what was written on the man's pad of paper. But he could not. Finally, the sky turned gray, then brightened. Just as the sun peeked over the horizon, the man awoke.

And then the Story did something that he hadn't done in a long, long time. He entered someone's thoughts. Not to speak, but, for once in his life, to listen.

The thoughts that he entered, of course, were the man's. It didn't take long for the Story to figure out that the man was coming from a meeting, that it was a meeting of astronomers, and that an extraordinary announcement had been made. Someone had detected planets outside the solar system. The planets were circling stars, just as the earth circles the star we call the sun. The Story knew from his recent travels that the universe was full of planets, but he could not fathom seeing one at such a distance. He listened on: the astronomers hadn't exactly *seen* the planets, not directly at any rate. What they had seen were stars leaning one way, then another—wobbling back and forth ever so slightly. They had also seen stars grow dim, then bright again, then dim, then bright—all at regular intervals.

The Story understood what those sightings meant. A star would wobble like that only if something were swinging around it, pulling it in one direction, then in the other. It would grow dim and bright in a regular way only if something were passing in front of it, something that didn't emit its own light. Something like a planet.

Not everyone at the meeting had agreed, however, that the mysterious objects circling those stars were planets. They could themselves be stars, the skeptics said. Brown dwarfs, perhaps. The discussion had gotten heated, and it had come down to this: what exactly is a planet? "Call them what you will," the man had said (he was just now saying it to himself again), "they are out there circling stars." Inwardly, he was certain: they were planets. But then, in his thoughts, he added, No big deal.

"No big deal?" stammered the Story. He couldn't believe his ears. And then he realized that he had entered a very strange mind.

Strange . . . but hard to leave. The Story crept in further—stealthily—until he came across a different line of thought. If you're going to speak a story, the man was saying, you have to know where you stand in space. You have to know where you stand in time.

I know where *I* stand, thought the Story of Everything. I'm on a planet circling a star in a remote corner of the universe. I'm out in the boondocks of space. He wouldn't have said that when he was young. When he was young, he would have said, I'm standing on solid ground, and everything else is circling *me*.

"That's where you stand in space," said the man. "But where do you stand in time?"

I stand outside of time, thought the Story.

The man got out his pad.

The Story didn't want to say a word, or even think a thought, that would alert the man to his presence, even though the man seemed perfectly aware of it. Right now the man was thinking about the "redshift" in light, the "Hubble constant," and "cosmic acceleration." Then it was the age of stars. Finally, the man said, "The universe is expanding. You can calculate backwards and figure out how old it is."

Fifteen billion years, thought the Story. He had heard the figure on his recent travels. But what did it have to do with him?

"Make it thirteen point seven," said the man. "And we're getting to that." He pointed to the letter M. "Matter appears on the first day, January 1. Maybe not in the very first instant, but you've got atoms within seconds. And in a matter of weeks, you've got galaxies and stars. The first generation of them."

"Within *seconds*?" blurted the Story of Everything. He couldn't help himself. "In a matter of *weeks*?" Then he realized what was happening. The man had taken the age of the universe and collapsed it into a single year.

"Right," said the man. He started flipping through pages. "The scale . . . here it is." The Story took a look.

Real Time	Time in Scale
13.7 billion years	= 1 year
1.1 billion years	= 1 month
37.5 million years	= 1 day
1.6 million years	= 1 hour
26 thousand years	= 1 minute

"There's the number to remember," said the man, pointing to the bottom line. "Twenty-six thousand years. In cosmic time, it's only a minute."

The Story was wondering where all this was going.

"I'll get to that." Now the man turned back to his original page. "Matter appears on January 1, but when does Life come in? The very first hints are found in rocks that are nearly four billion years old. That means that Life emerged sometime in September. On earth at least."

The Story had seen the very rocks the man was talking about. Embedded in them were the remains of one-celled creatures, very tiny but very real. Where does that leave me? he wondered.

"Okay, when is there evidence of something that could produce a story? When is there evidence of Spirit? Not until
December 31st. Not until the last day of the year. Not until the
last hour of the last day. Not until. . . ."

It was there on the pad:

S . . . December 31, 11:58 P.M.

Two minutes to midnight. Two minutes ago.

"Call it thought," said the man. "Or mind. Or intelligence.
Or consciousness. I call it Spirit. The question is: when is there
evidence of it? And where?"

If the Story had seen the evidence, he hadn't noticed.

"There's a cave in Africa, on its southern tip, where etchings
have been found. Patterns of triangles on an ochre stone. It looks
like they were put there by a thinking mind. It's a guess, a stretch
maybe, but suppose they were. Those triangles are seventy-five
thousand years old. 11:57 P.M. In a cave in France, there are
paintings of animals, beautiful paintings, that go back thirty-five
thousand years. Not a stretch at all. It's art, evidence of Spirit.
Nearby are flutes made of bone that go back thirty-two thousand
years. Music. We're under a minute and a half now. So let's say
there's evidence of Spirit—ballpark—fifty thousand years ago.
11:58 P.M."

What about me? the Story wondered again. He wasn't liking
the looks of this.

"Ah, yes. You. At a burial site in Russia there's a skeleton of a man wearing bracelets, necklaces, and a tunic with hundreds of ivory beads made from the tusks of mammoths. The burial took place twenty-eight thousand years ago. Imagine the ceremony that accompanied that burial. Imagine the beliefs that did. The earth had never seen anything like it."

The man paused, and grew more serious. "I have to believe there was a Story of Everything around the time of that burial. It would have been a spoken story because writing was a long way off. Writing is only a few seconds old, half a minute at the outside. So I'm guessing that a Story of Everything came into being on New Year's Eve, right around 11:59 P.M."

And that's where I stand in time? thought the Story of that name. That's it?

The man showed little compassion. "If Everything is a year old, you are just a minute old."

TWENTY-FOUR

JUICE?" The voice came from outside the man's head, and it startled the Story of Everything. "Eggs?" The airplane's cabin was stirring, and a breakfast cart was coming down the aisle. In an instant, the man's thoughts turned from the cosmos to coffee, and the Story was glad for it. He had just taken a blow, and he needed some time to recover. *Everything was bigger than its Story.* He had known that, but he had not comprehended the scale of it. He had not understood that everything was *that much* bigger, that everything had been in existence *that much* longer. The comparison was crushing.

I'll get used to it, the Story was telling himself as he left the man's thoughts and returned to his seat. He had gotten used to a lot of other things this past year. How distant his library seemed now! How distant the books that said, "You always were and you always will be."

The plane banked, sunlight streamed into the cabin, and the man got up to stretch his legs, brushing past the Story as he did. Now the Story sensed that there was something he would never get used to, something about the man, but what it was he couldn't exactly say. When the man returned, the Story decided to have another go inside his head.

He ended up in a place where complex ideas were flying around. Consciousness. Intelligence. Symbolic capacity. Abstract reasoning. Interiority. Transcendence. The words were so multisyllabic the Story had to duck. Further in, however, the air was calmer and the words shorter. Mind. Heart. Soul. God. Spirit. Further still, there were no words, only things to see. The Story came upon a garden that was nearly empty. On pebbles of stone, neatly raked, there lay three rocks, well spaced and in a row.

Spirit, Matter, Life, thought the Story of Everything.

"Matter, Life, Spirit," said the man.

The Story winced. That was it—the very thing he would never get used to. Not the words, but the *order* of the words. It was what the man put first: Matter, not Spirit.

The Story looked again at the garden. There were no signs there, no directions, no arrows. Nothing said that one of the rocks "led up" to another or "came down" to it. Nothing said that one was the mover, and the others the moved; or that one was the cause, and the others the effect. There was no indication that one of the rocks followed simple rules, and the others rules more complex. The garden didn't explain a thing. All it said was, Look.

Which is what the man was doing.

"Why did religion come first?" he asked all of a sudden. The word had rarely come up in his thoughts, but there it was. "I mean, why did religion come before science?" That was another word the man had rarely used.

Did it? wondered the Story of Everything. Did religion come before science? On his first journey through the cosmos, there was no "religion," there was no "science." The words didn't exist. But on his second trip, he had heard the words often. And he had noticed that the places of religion were older than the places of science. The texts of religion were older too. So much older that the arrival of science had caused a "revolution."

"I don't know," said the man.

Don't know what? thought the Story.

"Why religion came first."

The Story of Everything didn't know either. The question had never occurred to him.

It had occurred to the man, of course, and it must have occurred many times because he fell into a monologue that was unusually convoluted. "It's something about the dawn of consciousness," he said, but what it was he really didn't know. "What's it like for a planet to wake up? And to do it for the first time?" That was the hard part, the impossible part, the man said—to picture the first time. "I can't imagine a first awakening. I've tried to do it, but I cannot. It's not like getting up in the morning. When you get up in the morning, you put on history, like clothes. Every day. But the *first* time. . . ."

The man fell silent. "So now I wonder if it's inevitable. That when a planet wakes up, it naturally faces the awakening? As you naturally face the dawn? That consciousness, when born, turns first to consciousness? To religion? To Spirit?"

The Story of Everything had done none of this wondering.

"But suppose it had been the other way around," said the man. "Suppose that science had come first."

Nor had the Story done any of that supposing.

"Suppose that everyone in Galileo's time had known that the sun was at the center of things, and suppose that Galileo had said, no, God was? Who would have been the condemners in that case? Who the condemned?"

The Story recalled the Inquisition, the torture and the killing.

"And suppose that everyone in Darwin's time took it for granted that humans had come from 'lower' animals? And suppose Darwin had said, Look, there's something 'higher.' What if he had written *The Ascent of Man*, not *The Descent*?"

He'd have gotten his story backwards, thought the Story of Everything.

"No," said the man, "He'd have gotten his story frontwards."

The Story soon learned that, to the man, "frontwards" meant that you started everything with Matter. "Matter was there at the beginning, on the first day. Life came later. Spirit, just moments ago."

No, thought the Story of Everything. Spirit was there on the first day. It was the Creator. It was the mover, the cause, the designer. "Spirit comes first," he asserted with conviction. "It was present before there was Matter. Before there was Life. It was present at the beginning."

"How do you know?" asked the man. "You weren't there for the beginning."

"How do *you* know?" shot back the Story. "You weren't there either."

It was pure reaction, and it stunned the man. The thought seemed never to have occurred to him. The Story waited in silence to see what he would say. He wondered if the man always worked out ideas this way, by arguing with stories in his head. All along, the man had treated the Story like one of his own thoughts.

Finally, the man spoke. "You're right. I was late for the show. Very late. As a matter of fact, I just walked in. But religion was late too. So was science. So were you. You weren't there for the Words of creation . . . and I wasn't there for the Bang."

TWENTY-FIVE

THE plane flew on, riding the crest of a tailwind. There wasn't a hint of turbulence in the air, only a slight banking now and then as it sought its destination and brought its passengers to their destiny. Out of the man's thoughts again, the Story pictured the garden he had just seen. He looked over at the man. We're looking at the same three rocks, he thought, but you're sitting on one side of the garden and I'm sitting on the other. Frontwards to you, backwards to me.

The plane entered a second night and the pilot predicted an early arrival. In no time at all galaxies of light appeared down below: cities on the coastline. For several hours now, the Story had been wondering if he was sitting next to the source of the longing. It was all too bizarre, he thought: A stranger writes my initials. I get into his head. We start thinking to each other. We start talking to each other. He practically looks me in the eye, and all the while he acts as if I'm not even there.

The Story looked at the man once again. Was this the source I set out to find? No, he decided, it couldn't be. Longings didn't act the way the man had. They didn't argue. They didn't turn you upside down. They showed more respect than that, and at least a little love.

Now the plane was circling back into the teeth of the wind. The man will soon be home, the Story realized, but I will not. The Story had no place to go now, no thread to pick up, nothing to try next. By the time the plane was on the ground, he was in a panic. This may not be the source, he figured, but it's about as close as I'm going to get.

So the Story of Everything followed the man through the terminal and into the parking lot. It was late, but the man didn't drive home. He headed for the ocean instead. He left his car there, in a deserted lot by the beach. In the dark, waves were rushing in, bringing with them the smell of the distant sea. The man took off his shoes and socks, left them by the edge of the boardwalk, and began to hike along the pounding surf. He stopped to roll up the legs of his pants. All the while, the Story followed by his side, the sand feeling cool and refreshing under his feet.

"What's new?" asked the man. The sharp-edged crescent of a moon peeked out from behind a cloud.

The Story stopped. He wasn't "in" the man's thoughts now (he hadn't even tried to get in), so how did the man know he was there? Perhaps the man's thoughts were starting to come "out."

"What's new?" repeated the man.

Unable to come up with much of anything, the Story said, "Extrasolar planets." He didn't think it this time, he actually said it. Out loud. And as soon as he did, he thought, How dumb! It was the man who had told *him* about extrasolar planets! Or thought them to him, or whatever he had done. And it was the man who had added, "No big deal."

"No big deal," said the man once again. "Those planets have been circling those stars for a long, long time. They're really very old." He and the Story were walking again.

The Story tried a second time. In a telescope circling the earth, he had seen light that had come from the most distant regions of the universe. No astronomer had ever seen that light before. No human being had. It was altogether new.

"New to astronomers," said the man before the Story even finished. "Newly detected. But actually very old. That light left its source billions of years ago. Close to when the universe began."

It made the *news* for goodness sake, thought the Story. It didn't make the *olds*. He felt an itch in the back of his neck. What was the man getting at? What was his point?

"It's this. If you tell the Story frontwards, the old stuff comes out old, and the new stuff comes out new. New isn't what was just discovered. It's what just now *happened*."

The itch got worse. "Okay," said the Story, "what's new? What just now happened?"

The man didn't answer. Instead, he asked another question. "What's weird?"

Now the itch became a pain.

"I mean, what's the strangest thing in the cosmos? The oddest thing ever to happen?"

A thought popped into the Story's head. Why, he couldn't say. "Strings."

"Yes!" said the man. "Yes! Strings are very weird." He paused. "But not, of course, the weirdest thing there is."

The Story of Everything had heard about strings in the hallways of the particle accelerators he had visited. Quarks weren't the smallest things of all, some scientists were saying. "Strings" were, little strands of vibrating energy. No one, of course, had ever seen a string. They were purely hypothetical. But mathematics pointed to their existence, seemed, even, to demand their existence. In the hypothetical world of strings, there were more than three dimensions, more than four, if you included time. There were as many as eleven, seven of them curled up inside the four we knew. There were even, quite possibly, universes parallel to our own. And universes bubbling up beyond our visible horizon.

"You don't get much weirder than strings," said the Story of Everything.

The man walked in silence for a while, and then he said, "You'll get used to them. If they exist, of course. It won't take long to realize how commonplace they are. As commonplace as atoms. They're everywhere. They've been part of everything since practically forever."

Set up again, thought the Story.

The man kept on. "I'll tell you what's really weird. And new. Compassion. Not long ago, somewhere in the universe, compassion began to circle a star."

"Compassion?" said the Story of Everything. "Compassion?" To him, compassion had been around forever. He couldn't remember *not* knowing about compassion. "No big deal," he said, and he felt good saying it.

"It's no big deal if you tell the Story backwards. Tell it frontwards and you'll see how astonishing compassion is. How unpredictable a development. It's the strangest thing a universe could produce."

Telling the Story frontwards, as the man kept repeating, meant starting with Matter, not Spirit. "I know I was late for the show," he said. "I know I missed the beginning. But. . . ." He stopped and came at the *but* from a different direction. "I know that religion came first, but . . . why not let science *speak* first? Give science the first day." If you did, said the man, everything would then look different. The old would be old, the new would be new, the surprising turns surprising. "Listen to this. Space and time shoot out from a point. In a matter of seconds, a universe is formed. It expands and expands. It slows down, it speeds up. And then, in some remote corner, it drops a speck of consciousness. It spills a little subjectivity. A touch of soul. And with it, compassion. Weird, eh?"

The Story of Everything could hardly say no, not when the man put it like that.

The man was just warming up. "What existed before compassion was so contrary to it. What existed before was violent. Compassion was gentle. What existed before was devoid of soul.

Compassion required soul. And once there was soul, compassion said, 'Enter someone else's. In the midst of outer space, enter someone's inner space.'"

Compassion was just the tip of the iceberg, said the man. The universe was full of "anomalies" just like it. Baseball was circling a star, the very same star. Ballet was too. And *Sergeant Pepper's Lonely Hearts Club Band*. And *Thirty-Six Views of Mount Fuji*. Virtue was in orbit, vice was, truth and lies. All of these things, so foreign to the universe, were circling a single star. How strange they were! How odd that the cosmos should produce them! And out of hydrogen!

"So much falls into place if you tell the Story frontwards," continued the man. Other speakers of the Story—the man acknowledged that there were many others—liked to say that science had "demoted" humans. It had stripped them of "illusions." It had struck a blow to "hubris." Our earth was the center of nothing, the other speakers said, nor was it designed with humans in mind. Humans were a chance event, an accident, a twig on the side of the tree of life, not its crown.

"Unless," said the man, "you start the Story differently. Unless you give the first day to Matter. Then there are no demotions. There is no shattering of illusion. There are no blows to hubris. Humans look like an accident, but one that was waiting to happen. Compassion comes out of the blue."

The man pointed down the coastline. "Look at all the sand on this beach. Suppose we came across a grain of sand, a single grain, that talked. How improbable would that be? How improbable that it existed? How improbable that we found it? One grain of sand is not the center of anything. But when one starts to talk, you've got to listen. You've got to ask what's going on. I don't know what's going on, but I do know this: a talking planet is rare. Rare beyond calculation."

"There must be others like it," said the Story of Everything. He was looking down the coastline, too, to where it disappeared. "There must be other grains of sand that talk, other signs of Spirit."

"Must be?" said the man. "We haven't found a one yet, not a single one. And we've been looking very, very hard. The movies make it look easy, but it isn't like the movies. This isn't *Star Trek*. It isn't *Star Wars*. It isn't special effects. And it's not like Europeans crossing an ocean five hundred years ago. The Europeans never left their grain of sand."

"But there must be . . . ," said the Story.

"You don't change a story until you know for sure. All I know is what just now happened. All I know is where the cosmos is right now. Not at the beginning. Not at the end. But somewhere in the middle, two minutes after a most remarkable turn of events."

The Story, who had held up rather well on this long, demanding walk, was now beginning to tire. His mind was tiring too, and wandering through memories of moon and sand and water. "Frontwards" and "backwards" were evoking distant images.

Suddenly the Story saw a carved-out stump and a boy who liked to turn things upside down. He saw the boy, stricken with grief, sitting there without a story. And then he recognized the man.

"Adam!" The shock in his voice was audible.

Adam froze. This time he knew that the voice he heard was not his own. A moment later, he knew whose it was. In a matter of seconds, Adam's whole life passed before him.

He turned to the Story of Everything. "Why did you leave?" he asked.

In shame, the Story spoke the truth. "I didn't have an answer."

TWENTY-SIX

EVERYTHING was different after that brief exchange. The Story felt a new remorse, and a deeper one. How many times would he have to say it? I was wrong. I was wrong, I was wrong, I was wrong. How many times had he said it already?

He had been wrong, in the time of Galileo, not to look in the telescope. He had been wrong, in the time of Darwin, to cede so much of himself. He had been wrong, just a while back, to believe that cyberspace could save him. But this was a different kind of wrong, and it caused a deeper pain.

The Story of Everything looked back on a life of being wrong, and he grew very, very weary. It's more than my form that needs to change, he realized. It's my very self. It's *me*.

In the days that followed, days of late summer sun, the Story of Everything became something of a beachcomber, and Adam became something of a homebody. The two never spoke again. The Story was now convinced that he had found the source of the longing. But he was just as convinced that he could never change as Adam wanted. Yes, he could do a better job with scale. Yes, he could acknowledge where he was standing, and when. Yes, he could even admit that he was late for the show, that he had missed the Words of creation. But he could never let science speak first. He could never give the first day to Matter. The place of honor belongs to Spirit, he said. At least in me.

There was more. Walking beside the sea each day, watching wave after wave come in, the Story kept seeing all the generations of people who had put their faith in him. Who had copied him, printed him, set up websites for him, defended him, died for him, even killed for him—just as he was. With his beginning where it was and his ending where it was. How could he turn his back on them now? How could he change on them, even if he wanted to? How could he ask their forgiveness?

I'm only a story, he told himself. I'm not God. I'm not the cosmos. I'm just a story. I came into being on a single grain of sand. I thought I would last forever, but I will not. My books said "always" to me: they lied. The computer promised eternity: it lied as well.

The truth, he said, is that I'm part of a universe in which things come and go. To be a thing that comes. . . . And here his thoughts would go no further.

One night the Story had a dream. He saw a river come out of the mountains and embark on a long, long journey. Where to, the dream didn't say, although the river had to get there. The river widened out in the plains, but after many days in the sun, it began to grow weak. It broke into little streams that wound their way around mounds of sand and rock. It had entered a desert. When the river saw where it was, it panicked, and the Story of Everything awoke from his sleep with a start.

The dream came back the following night, and the night after that, and for many, many nights after that. It was always the same. The river would leap from the mountains, broaden out in the plains, and diminish to a trickle in the desert. Then it would panic, and the Story of Everything would sit up alert, unable to breathe.

TWENTY-SEVEN

ADAM, for his part, had walked away from the Story after their words on the beach. The memories had been too much for him. All the searching he had done. All the places that had come up empty. And then that shameful excuse: "I didn't have an answer."

He should have known, of course. He should have known that the Story had been with him on that plane. Never in Adam's life had patterns flowed so readily. Never had details come so quickly. With the Story in his thoughts, Adam had felt like Copernicus must have felt (he actually said that to himself). How long, he wondered, had the Story been following him? Been beside him? Been "in" his thoughts?

The irony of it all, thought Adam, thinking back to a cool desert morning: The story that a ray of sun had told him to speak turned out to be *this* Story, with *this* sordid past and *this* flawed nature. This nature so deeply flawed.

The irony left Adam angry, and in the face of his anger his thinking collapsed. Gone was the flow he had felt on the plane. Gone were the patterns, gone the detail. All the calculations he had made, all the dating of events, all the simple reversals couldn't stand up to his anger. Nothing would stay where he put it.

Nor would anything stand up to his guilt. Each time Adam touched a piece of the Story, he would see the hill where the oak once stood. He would see his grandfather's face. And he would ask, How can I take the words of a man I love and turn them upside down? How can I tell his Story backwards? An eerie thought came, a frightening thought: what if my grandfather had been there, too, there on the plane and there on the beach, listening in on my thoughts? Actually hearing the betrayal?

One night Adam had a dream. He saw the nighttime sky he had loved as a child, with Polaris in place, and the Dippers, and the Bear, and the Lion. Pegasus was there, looking for a rider. Taurus was dreaming of far-off Crete. Orion had his eye on the Scorpion. All as it should be.

Then something terrible happened.

Alien stars appeared on the horizon, a few at first, then hordes. They invaded the sky like a swarm of ants. All the constellations crumbled, and all the stories too. The stars became a frenzied mob, filled with panic, racing toward. . . . Adam woke up.

The dream came back the next night, and the night after that, and for many, many nights thereafter. It was always the same. The stars would be where they'd always been, and then the invasion would begin. Alien stars would overrun the sky and every constellation would be lost. The very sky would panic, and Adam would sit up alert, unable to breathe.

TWENTY-EIGHT

IT was a matter of dying, then: the Story of Everything could see that now. He knew that his own journey was coming to an end. The only question left was where. Where was he to die? Perhaps I can pick the place, he thought.

And then the Story recalled a place he had once seen in Adam, an out-of-the-way place far from the empty garden. He recalled how branches of pine lay scattered in that place. He recalled how green things were, all around. He recalled the sorrow that he saw, and the anger, and the guilt. And then he felt the love.

The Story knew at once that he could trust this place. No matter what had happened in the past, he knew it would receive him.

And so the Story left the beach and found his way back to Adam. Without saying a word, he entered Adam's thoughts for the very last time.

Once he saw the branches of pine, the Story of Everything was overcome with sleep. He lay down, closed his eyes, and let the earth come over him. That night he had his final dream. When the river came to the desert, a wind began to blow. It was a soothing wind, and for the first time in the dream, the river didn't panic. For the first time, it heard the wind say, "I will lift you up."

TWENTY-NINE

THAT night Adam dreamt as well. When the sky began to panic, clouds came in and covered it, clouds so thick and low that he could hardly breathe. It began to rain.

Adam stood in the rain. As it came over him, he felt a cleansing. Something said, I forgive. And something else, I am forgiven.

The clouds left slowly, like a curtain rising. When the trailing edge had passed, Adam saw a nighttime sky that he had never seen before. It was clear and deep and dark and radiant. There were stars as far as the eye could see, billions of stars, each precisely placed, each precisely lit. And all the stars, in all their clarity and depth, formed but a single structure. One sky, one constellation. It all came together.

Adam stared into that sky for a long, long time. It was the kind of dream you never want to wake up from, the kind you remember for the rest of your life.

THIRTY

THAT fall was one of the warmest in years, and when Thanksgiving came around, Adam set out for a family gathering in the very house where he had grown up. A new generation was living there, but the family's way of life was still intact. And now, for the first time in a long time, a big reunion had been planned.

Adam had said he was coming, and so had Jamie, and so, to everyone's surprise, had Elise. For Elise, it was a chance to see Adam again, and even more, to see the place where *it* had happened. She remembered Adam's words: "That's where he told me the Story of Everything." She remembered her reply: "It was *only* a Story." A fateful word, she often told herself in the years that followed.

Elise had seen her share of success in life, and probably more than her share, but time had not erased the taste of the early years, nor the taste of the man who had been a part of them. Her marriage had been a good one, but nothing like that first year with Adam. There were things she had taken from him that year, things that she kept to herself and turned to in difficult times, things she continued to love.

Jamie was in his thirties now, his career at a crossroads, or perhaps a standstill. Decisions had to be made, but they could wait. What couldn't wait, in Jamie's mind, was this event. He had two children, they were growing fast, and they had seen far too little of their grandfather. It was now or never, he thought. They had to get to know this man.

The younger of Jamie's children was a boy of seven who seemed to be everywhere at once, running, climbing, shouting, scheming, collecting friends. An open book, said Elise, a lot like his father. His sister Dawn was another matter altogether. She was only ten, but already there was something in her that seemed so far away. The look in her eyes, perhaps, or maybe the frown on her face, something not quite of this world. She had a way of getting absorbed in things, and a love of solitude unusual in a child her age. She could spend hours at her sketches, or at her collections, laying things out one way, then another. She could be intensely affectionate one minute, then disappear the next. She could ask you question after question, each one stranger than the one before, and walk away unsatisfied with every one of your answers. What was she after? you would wonder. And you would feel helpless. And then you'd find her sitting in front of a computer, or with her nose in a book. And when she was done, she'd look you straight in the eye and tell you everything was fine. And you wouldn't have a clue.

Jamie didn't know what it was about his daughter, but Elise did. She knew because she had seen it before.

Adam was the last to arrive that Thanksgiving, and so the last to remark how much older the children (but not, of course, the grownups) looked. At dinner, everyone seemed to be talking at once, but by the next morning things had quieted down. When the sun came out that afternoon, lighting up trees barren of leaves, Adam slipped out the back door to do some exploring. Elise noticed—and knew. She found Dawn and told her to catch up with her grandfather. "He wants to show you around," she whispered.

Adam heard the door slam, and then he heard a frantic "Wait!" He turned and did as he was told. The young lady charging after him would not be denied this contact. A young Elise, Adam thought, but no, she was different from Elise. He wished he had seen more of her.

"Grandma said you wanted to show me around."

"How did she know?" Adam replied.

They were standing in dry brown grass at the edge of the orchard. It was smaller than Adam remembered. The trees had been replaced long ago, but the same mix seemed to be there. Apples, cherries, plums. Maybe a peach or two.

Adam picked an apple off the ground, studied it, and handed it to Dawn. Dawn looked it over, then put it in a pocket. So many memories were coming back to Adam that he began to tell his granddaughter about the time he had spent in the orchard—about the veins he had found in the petals of a flower, about the stick-people, about his trips to the library to find out what they were.

Dawn peppered him with questions. What were the veins *for*? What did the stamens *do*? What kind of library *was it*? None of the questions seemed strange to Adam, and when he answered them, Dawn was satisfied.

They moved on to the creek, which was nearly dry, and followed it until they found a shallow pool. Adam started turning over rocks. Dawn took off her shoes and socks, splashed into the creek, and started helping him.

Finally he found a rock with a tube attached to its bottom. He broke it open.

"Oooh!" said Dawn. "That is so-o-o-o cool!" She held the little white worm between her fingers. "Where did it come from?"

Now Adam told her the story of the caddis fly. How the worm hatched from an egg in the bottom of the creek and built itself a house. How it left that house and rose to the surface of the water, then into the air. How it flew for a few glorious days. How it mated, laid its eggs in the creek, and died.

By the time she had dried her feet (she used the top of her socks) and put on her shoes, Adam had spotted the tracks of a deer, hardened in some mud. He and Dawn tried to follow them, but it wasn't easy. She kept on chattering. Finally, when they were standing at a neighbor's fence and reaching out to touch a horse (they had forgotten about the deer), Dawn ran out of questions. She grew silent, and Adam let the silence be. The horse left its side of the fence, and Adam pointed out a hill that he wanted to explore.

It had changed over the years. Where one majestic tree had stood, now many did. And that, thought Adam, was as it should be. The stump was gone, too, and Adam was glad for that as well. He would rather remember the fallen tree with children sitting on its limbs in twos and threes, the way they were in a photograph he had somewhere.

Dawn found an outcropping of sandstone and sat down. Adam noticed a seashell, but before he could point it out, Dawn's eyes got a certain look, and her face got a certain frown, and she addressed her grandfather directly.

"Why," she asked, "did you turn over so many rocks when you were a boy? How did you find the stick-people?"

The sun was getting low in the sky, but a warm breeze was still blowing, no doubt mistaking the season. Adam let a gust pass, and then he said, "I was looking for a Story."

And then it all came out.

It started with the tree. Adam showed Dawn exactly where it stood, exactly where it fell, exactly where he sat to hear the Story. He told his granddaughter about the man who told the Story, and how they found his body in the snow, and how the Story disappeared, and how it returned.

And then, because the time had come, Adam told Dawn the Story of Everything. He told it to her his way—frontwards, with Matter on the first day, though he wasn't there to see it. Out from a point it came—atoms, galaxies and stars, one generation, a second, and on the Story flowed, the great and small of it, the great and small of Matter, Adam losing track of what he was saying, only aware of his granddaughter's eyes absorbing. Earth came into being—it was August of the cosmic year—a place for Speakers of the Story. Life emerged: bacteria and genes, dinosaurs with parrot beaks, fish with horns, plants with mouths. *A*'s and *c*'s and *g*'s and *t*'s. The changing of the species, Life where you'd least expect it. When Adam looked up and saw the first stars of night, he began to feel as though he were telling the Story to the universe itself. He came to November of the cosmic year, and then December, and then the last few days, the last few hours, the last few minutes. He got to what was circling stars, to what was circling ours. The grain of sand that talked, baseball, and compassion—Spirit, rising out of Matter, rising out of Life. Everything evolving. He looked at Dawn. "You are the Story's surprise," he said. "You come from stardust."

"I do?" Her concentration broke; she got that frown of hers. "But how?"

"I wish I knew."

"Me too."

In the quiet that followed, Adam could almost see his grand-daughter's mind at work, turning the Story over and over. Suddenly, she bolted upright. "I think I know," she said. "When the dust was ready, Spirit . . . like . . . breathed into it."

"But how did Spirit get there?"

"It didn't *get* there, it was *always* there," said Dawn. "It had to wait, that's all." And that is how she took the Story in.

It was over now. Neither Dawn nor Adam said a word, but both of them knew that the telling had come to an end. Adam, however, had one thing left to say. He told Dawn the Story would have to change one day. He didn't know when, he didn't know how, he didn't know why. All he knew was that change was coming.

Dawn said, "I like the Story just the way it is."

Adam had to smile. He had liked the Story, too, just the way it was when he first heard it. But things had happened in his life, and things had happened in the world, and the Story had to be changed. His eyes moistened when he told Dawn that when he lost the Story, he never stopped looking for it, not really at any rate, and that if she ever lost it, she must not stop either, not ever, no matter what.

"I'm not going to lose it," she said.

Adam repeated himself. "If you lose the Story, you must never stop looking for it. Not ever."

Dawn was in a thoughtful mood as they found their way down through the darkness and headed home for dinner. Adam was torn. He knew his granddaughter had given her heart to the Story, but he worried that the day would come when she and the Story would part. Maybe it would ask too much of her. Maybe she would tire of it, or maybe she'd grow angry, as he had done. Maybe it would beg for change, and she'd refuse. Whatever her struggles (Adam couldn't bear to think of them), they would be different from his. In the end, however (he knew this too), the

Story would die in her and then be born again. And she would be its Speaker.

Was it a blessing or a curse, what had happened on the hill? Adam couldn't say. He only knew that it was meant to be, and that he could not help this child with what she had to do.

Dawn remained silent all the way back to the house. From the back porch you could see lights shining brightly inside and food steaming on the kitchen stove. People were talking again, and getting in each other's way. As Adam opened the screen door, Dawn took one of his hands and tugged on it with both of hers. "Grandpa," she said, "let's go there again tomorrow."

AFTERWORD

He it was who gave me sure knowledge of what exists,
to understand the structure of the world
and the action of the elements,
the beginning, end and middle of the times,
the alternation of the solstices
and the succession of the seasons,
the cycles of the year and the position of the stars,
the natures of animals and the instincts of wild beasts,
the powers of spirits and human mental processes,
the varieties of plants and the medical properties of roots.
And now I understand everything, hidden or visible,
for Wisdom, the designer of all things, has instructed me.

THESE words come from a book called *Wisdom*, which was written in the Egyptian city of Alexandria over two thousand years ago, in the first century BCE. Alexandria at the time was a place where art, philosophy, religion, medicine, and science—all the knowledge that then existed—came together and stirred deep passions. East and West met there. Cultures clashed there. Euclid created geometry there. Cleopatra took her life there. A huge library existed there, with half a million papyrus scrolls. It was there that a voice cried out in the desert, claiming that the earth circled the sun. (No one listened.) And it was there that the Bible was first translated in its entirety, from Hebrew into Greek.

About the author of *Wisdom* we know only that he was a devout Jew who wrote in Greek and did so in the voice of the great sage Solomon. His work, however, was never incorporated into the Hebrew canon. Instead, it found a place in the Bible of one of the Christian denominations, the Roman Catholic.

The author of *Wisdom* attributed his understanding of everything to two sources: God, the "He" in the passage above, and Wisdom, who is a "She." In many parts of the Bible, God and Wisdom are pictured as working in tandem. The Book of Proverbs says that Wisdom was with God from the very beginning of time. She acted as a partner (a "confidant," in one translation) when He laid the foundations of the earth. In *Wisdom* we read of a quality of Hers that is central to the story I have told. Though God grants knowledge that is sure and certain, Wisdom is "quicker to move than any motion."

WHAT THE
PARABLE MEANS

R EADING a parable is only half the experience; what remains is the question *What does it mean?* To work on that, I invite you to The-Story-of-Everything Place (www.thestoryofeverything.com). Here you can ask questions, post observations, download (and add to) a discussion guide, make arrangements for your class or reading group, receive blogs on science and spirituality, or simply contact me. See how a community and a commentary develop around specific passages in the book.

As the Story itself realized in Chapter 15, we live with one foot in the print era and another in the electronic era. Print has now done its job. To complete the parable experience, we turn next to electronics. What about you and *The Story of Everything*?

ABOUT THE
AUTHOR

J OHN KOTRE is the author of eight books about lives, memories, and legacies, all of which take a narrative approach. Best known for his work on "generativity"—the impact of one's life on future generations—Kotre was also the creator of the award-winning public television and radio series *Seasons of Life*.

A onetime Jesuit seminarian, Kotre received his Ph.D. in psychology from the University of Chicago and spent thirty-five years as a professor and project director at the Dearborn and Ann Arbor campuses of the University of Michigan. He and his wife, Kathy, have a blended family of five adult children and six grandchildren. They live in Ann Arbor, Michigan.

You can learn more about Kotre and his work by visiting www.johnkotre.com. More on his first venture into the field of science and religion is available at www.thestoryofeverything.com.